Women Seen and Heard is a mighty ......
book that provides "lessons learned" by effective spea....
and advocates—some inspiring, some practical—that can
help all of us to be more influential.

—**Anita Roddick OBE, Founder of
The Body Shop and author of
*Business as Unusual***

Finding your voice is one of the most valuable treasures in
life. This book teaches you to use it to help others!

—**Congresswoman Loretta Sanchez**

Women Seen and Heard is for every woman who wants to
be heard in the boardroom, the public square, or anywhere
the traffic in great ideas is blocked by the bottleneck of
sexist notions. Ferguson and Phillips have written the
book on speaking truth to power.

—**Gloria Feldt, President Planned
Parenthood Federation**

This book prepares women with the attitude, tools and
role models necessary to exert their influence when they
are speaking "as the voice of authority."

—**Heather Cameron, Vice President and
General Manager, Western Sales and
Account Management Division
Thomson-West**

Women Seen and Heard offers advice for becoming
stronger public speakers in a way that shows us how to
build on, rather than abandon, our unique strengths,
values and personalities.

—**Professor Martha McCaughey, Ph.D.,
Director of Women's Studies,
Appalachian State University**

Women Seen and Heard: Lessons Learned from Successful Speakers

Dear Diane —
Warmest regards,
Lois Phillips

Lois Phillips, Ph.D. and Anita Perez Ferguson, M.A.

Luz Publications

WOMEN SEEN AND HEARD:
Lessons Learned from Successful Speakers
by Lois Phillips, Ph.D. and Anita Perez Ferguson, M.A.

Published by:

Luz Publications

Copyright © 2004 Lois Phillips and Anita Perez Ferguson

Publisher's Cataloging-in-Publication
(Provided by Quality Books, Inc.)
Phillips, Lois,
    Women seen and heard : lessons learned from successful speakers /
Lois Phillips and Anita Perez Ferguson.
    p. cm.
    Includes bibliographical references.
    ISBN 0-9673300-5-0

    1. Public speaking for women. 2. Women in public life—United States.
3. Leadership in women—United States. 4. Race discrimination—
United States. 5. Sex discrimination against women—United States.
6. Social advocacy. I. Ferguson, Anita Perez. II. Title.
PN4192.W65P45 2004   909.5'1'082
    QBI33–1443

                    10 9 8 7 6 5 4 2 3 1

            womenseenandheard@yahoo.com

            Editor: Gail M. Kearns
        Cover Design: Diego Linares
Book Design and Typography: Cirrus Design
    Book Production: Penelope C. Paine

Printed in the United States of America

Contents

Preface

From Lois:

Like many others growing up in the fifties and sixties, I lacked contemporary female role models. Women in the news were as different from one another as Eleanor Roosevelt was from Twiggy. Jacqueline Kennedy's charm and glamour made the front-page and yet, while her ideas were intelligent, her breathless voice wasn't a style that I wanted to emulate. I preferred the more direct style of news anchors and secretly harbored a desire to enter the field of broadcast journalism. But, lacking female role models, I soon gave up that dream and began to drift through adolescence.

A typical New Yorker, I was always gregarious with my peers and enjoyed the company of lively people. By the time I entered Queens College, I spoke a mile a minute. Conversations with my best friend on the phone would have been unintelligible to anyone else. This may have been fine in high school, but once I began my college studies majoring in speech communication, it became clear that I needed help. I was initially very intimidated by the eloquent and engaging faculty and by the poise of my peers, but they would soon become positive role models for me. At some point, I had enough confidence to focus my studies in the area of rhetoric, which helped me learn classical theories of persuasion and also develop a public persona through public speaking skills.

Over the years, I've been very grateful for my rigorous classical education. It made me realize that I could think, solve problems, and articulate my own theories about why situations in life happen the way they do. The skills and knowledge about how to speak to groups came in handy later on when I needed to think on my feet, deal with a difficult audience, or debate a controversial issue. Presentation skills have also helped me transition through many professional changes, from the classroom to the boardroom.

During the seventies, inspired by the writings and speeches of Betty Friedan and Gloria Steinem, I became an activist with regard to women's access to education. With encouragement from a women's group in the Connecticut River Valley and using the persuasive speaking skills learned in college, I convinced a dean at the University of Massachusetts Amherst to give me a desk and a phone to test the need for a new continuing education program for returning women students. As a result, the program was soon funded and established. In California, armed with the confidence from that earlier effort, I was hired to mount a new branch of a national university. Although I had a minuscule budget to produce a certain level of enrollment, I was able to quickly recruit students and accumulate the necessary numbers. My presentation skills allowed me to confidently market the program to business groups, professional associations, and institutional leaders and build a financially viable campus. Later, in my thirties, I produced two local cable television shows and was able to feel comfortable facing the cameras while interviewing celebrities like Jane Fonda, as well as civic and business leaders. I couldn't have done any of this without knowing how to present my ideas to an audience and think on my feet.

Many extraordinary and accomplished people pass the microphone to the less competent members of their team or group who have no hesitancy about speaking up. When this happens, the audience loses out by not gaining the benefits of the best person's wisdom, and the group loses out because their ideas aren't well represented. This situation doesn't have to happen. People *can* overcome feelings of stage fright. The skills aren't difficult to learn, once you decide you're ready.

I once taught a ten-week class called "Public Speaking for Women." The re-entry students in the class came with varying degrees of sophistication and a variety of life and work experiences. But they all had one thing in common: they were terrified of getting up and giving a presentation, much less a speech. Because the class was small, we had the luxury of being able to dwell on speechmaking as a developmental process and give feedback within a supportive environment. By the end of the ten weeks, each speaker's progress was visible to all of us, captured on videotape.

At the end of the semester, each student made a point of telling me how empowering it was to be able to confidently communicate the ideas, beliefs, and feelings that mattered most, whether to a small group or large audience. One shy student, Mary, who was seeing a therapist at the time, made particularly dramatic improvement over ten weeks. She told me that the course had given her self-confidence which spilled over into her personal life, and that she and her therapist believe it had exponentially moved her therapy forward. It made perfect sense. Mary had found her "voice"—not just the ability to express ideas and project her voice, but the confidence that came when one exercises the right to free speech. She had realized that it was both emotionally and professionally costly to remain silent. She had learned that she needed to be able to clearly express her feelings in order to relate to others, and that it didn't help to be defensive about them. The students' personal growth was inspiring. As a result, I came to believe that mastery of presentation skills—or public speaking—not only builds self-confidence and self-esteem in general but that it is a positive adjunct to conventional forms of therapy. Public speaking is empowering.

Since then, I have coached women lawyers, doctors, managers, technical personnel, authors on book tours, and new politicians, helping them learn to speak up and be heard. I have seen firsthand how reticent individuals can quickly overcome their dread of public speaking once they find the motivation to do so. Perhaps more interesting is the fact that presenters can transfer this newfound self-confidence to social relationships and business settings.

In some cultures, the idea of a woman asserting herself is a ridiculous if not an insulting idea, one that violates religious fundamentalism. Recall the images of Afghani women in burkhas, silenced by an oppressive fundamentalist group that forbade them basic rights—including the right to have a public voice. Women's status in American society may be very different, but when Sherron Watkins, vice president of Enron Corporation, initially tried to warn the CEO of improprieties, she was silenced. Later she told her side of the story in a congressional hearing and to the media. Today she is a sought after public speaker because people want to hear her side of the story. We see creative changes occur within every sector of society when women have become effective advocates for policy changes in the workplace, in government, and in their communities.

Whether you have a story to tell or an idea to sell, this book is designed for women who want to be seen and heard so that they can create real changes for others.

From Anita:

Advice on how to speak clearly and convincingly is all around us. Finding confidence in your ideas and your own genuine voice is the homework of every aspiring female leader. When I had a chance to collaborate on *Women Seen and Heard*, I began to recall all the mentors, methods, and myths I had encountered during my years as a trainer, candidate, advocate and political appointee in Washington, D.C., and around the world. Those lessons are in this book.

Former Governor Ann Richards was speaking to a group of women activists. She described the need for clarity in all presentations. She said, "If you can't explain a public policy in terms that your mama can understand, then you haven't got it right."

Being clear and knowing when to speak up and when to shut up is still not easy. I do trust my instincts, now that I have more experience, but I rely on tested techniques like asking specific questions that show me how to be fair and thoughtful without sharing my opinion too early:

> *Can you tell me more about how you'd rank these priorities? What do you identify as the best possible outcome for this project? How would you describe the budget impact of your idea?*

Sitting next to U.S. Senator Dianne Feinstein during a meeting with environmentalists, I noticed that she was quickly scribbling numbers as this group described their plan. At the end of their complex presentation, she went right to the heart of the matter. "What you're telling me is that by spending one-tenth of a percent more on water processing per year, we can clean up the drinking water for our entire state," she summarized. She had worked the numbers and was able to make the very point that should have been the group's opening statement.

With Senator Feinstein's example in mind, I often teach women to remember three steps in order to rise to leadership:

1) Read up on your subject.

2) Write out, document, and publish your opinion or position.

3) Work the numbers to make your case.

Women Seen and Heard is as much about the time spent preparing to speak in public as it is about actually standing behind the podium, microphone in front of your mouth. Long before you stand before the audience, the speech process begins. Knowing your topic, having a special perspective, and being able to relate that to a particular group or individual is a challenging task. When your career, cause, or community is depending on you, you've got to be ready for the pressure.

Women Seen and Heard takes you behind the scenes to hear about those outrageous moments that occur before you get to the podium. Even lessons on last-minute preparation are important. I can't tell you how many times, prior to an interview, I've subtly scanned a waiting room or reception area for last-minute insights about what a potential donor or supporter may be thinking the day of our appointment. I do the same with a large audience, eavesdropping in the hallways or even the restroom, reading the conference agenda and surveying the audience for clues. "Doesn't everyone do this?" I once asked a colleague. "Well, no," she admitted. "As a matter of fact, I am usually so nervous, I hide out in my room until just before my speech is due. I never know what I'm walking into!"

I believe *Women Seen and Heard* is what many women have been hungering for—an open and honest support group composed of women speakers, shedding their designer jackets and saying, "Okay, here's how I really do it." Every woman interviewed for *Women Seen and Heard* shares some helpful suggestion for getting speakers through tough interviews and meetings as well as facing potentially hostile audiences.

We've all heard the suggestion about imagining your audience naked in order to overcome your fear of public speaking. Dottie Walters, a professional speaker and coach, once offered one piece of advice that I thought distinguished her attitude and personality. When she's behind the podium, Dottie imagines that she has a tray of goodies baked up for her audience, and during her speech she is distributing the very items that each person has been hungering for.

Speaking? It's easy, or so I've always thought. Contributing to *Women Seen and Heard* has given me a new appreciation for the skills and talents that make me a leader and help me make a living. But, more importantly, it has helped me to acknowledge all the other people who have helped me with advice and a strong example.

Your voice is a gift on many levels. May you celebrate the joy of being a woman who is "seen and heard."

Acknowledgments

We wish to express special thanks to our spouses, Bill Ferguson and Dennis Thompson, and to Tracy Phillips, and Craig Phillips, for their encouragement and belief in the importance of this project. Lois wishes to acknowledge Jinny Webber, Barbara Lindemann, Holly Teliska, Janice Rubin Rudestam, David Ewald, and Ilene Segalove for their assistance at critical junctures in the research as well as the writing, rewriting, and editing process. Gail Kearns served us well as technical editor and Chris Nolt of Cirrus Design contributed expert design assistance. Penny Paine guided us through the publication process. Friends and colleagues who participated in a peer review process included Nancy Franco, Fran Lotery, Ph.D., Tina Kistler, Eva Menkin, Barbara Mintzer, Linda Powell, Ph.D., Susan Rose, D. Merilee Clunis, Ph.D., Sara Miller McCune, and Sarah Greenberg.

The following individuals participated in research or administrative internships or provided staff support along the way: Aimee Olivera, Leslie Shinkel, Leigh Fullmer, Vicki Godlewski, Jennifer Gann, and Margot Lauren Dement. Publisher Mindy Bingham was encouraging throughout the process.

We appreciate the time that conference speakers were willing to spend being interviewed about their public speaking experiences, and they are quoted throughout the book. They are extremely intelligent, articulate, dedicated women leaders whose advocacy and spokesperson role required that they speak to the media, groups, and large conference audiences. The interviews were the galvanizing force behind the book and were conducted with communications author and women's health advocate Susan Lowell Butler; Ida Castro, attorney and former director of the EEOC; Janice Weinman, former director of AAUW; Angela Oh, attorney and journalist appointed to the White House Commission on Race; Betsy Myers, former director of the White House Office of Women and now director of Alumni Relations at the JFK School at Harvard; Marie Wilson, director of the Ms. Foundation; Liz Carpenter, author and former press secretary to Lady Bird Johnson; Laura Groppe, CEO of GirlGames; Geraldine Jensen, CEO of ACES; Kathleen Drennan, CEO of Women's Health Initiative; Ann Stone, Republicans for Choice, commentator, and trainer; Congresswoman Loretta Sanchez, 47th Congressional District of California; and former Superintendent of California Instruction, Delaine Eastin.

We thank Professor Martha McCaughey, Ph.D., director of Women's Studies, Appalachian State University, Heather Cameron, vice president and general manager, Western Sales and Account Management Division Thomson-West Publishing Company and Anita Roddick for their endorsements of *Women Seen and Heard: Lessons Learned from Successful Speakers.*

Section One

THE POLITICS OF
SPEAKING

CHAPTER 1

Introduction and Overview

Is gender still an issue for women speakers in gaining the voice of authority? *Women Seen and Heard: Lessons Learned from Successful Speakers* will tell you that the answer is a resounding "Yes." In the twenty-first century, society needs to resolve some tough and controversial issues that dramatically affect women, and women's voices need to be included in the debates and discussions that matter. Health care, social security, housing, safe schools as well as domestic violence, equity in the workplace, and reproductive choice are complex issues that are out on the table. And women demand a place at the table, not just a level playing field, in order to present a woman's perspective.

You don't need to be an heiress, a CEO, or an elected official to have power and authority. You can leverage the personal power you have and move groups and audiences to action by being articulate and eloquent. Presentation skills are empowering.

Women, as outsiders within the establishment, have less investment in maintaining the status quo and, therefore, can ask those challenging questions. Perhaps it's not surprising that *Time* magazine gave the 2003 Person of the Year award to three women who had the courage to speak up about what they saw as unethical practices. Although their employers did not take them seriously at first, ultimately each woman was able to tell her story in her own way to the government and to the press.

Young women today believe that they can be anything they want to be, and why not? They certainly have a wider range of options than their mothers did. But the truth is that more women function in the role of homemaker *and* bread-winner, bringing home the bacon and cooking it too. Yes, diverse women may well be breaking new ground every day, but—and this is critical to understand—not in numbers large enough to form a critical mass. As a result, age-old stereo-types about women persist and affect how audiences perceive speakers. Women managers, advocates, professionals, and community leaders must be aware of how stereotypes persist even at a non-conscious level and, more to the point, how stereotypes can sabotage women's effectiveness at the podium. The audience is wondering: *Can she deliver on the promises she's made? Can she broker power? Is she tough enough for the job?* Simply put, audiences are more critical of women speakers than men, and if women don't answer these ques-tions up front, they will not succeed in their role as speaker.

At the podium, gaining credibility as a leader is critical, but—historically speaking—credibility is men's to lose and women's to win. Men start with credibility but certainly can lose it by delivering a deadly dull presentation. Throughout history women have been all but ignored for their insights and accomplishments. Sure, there are some notable excep-tions—but "the quotable woman" is a fairly modern phe-nomenon. Let's take a quick look back.

For centuries, the voice of authority has been a male voice. The voice of the Catholic Church, as well as most major religious groups, is certainly male. American presi-dents have always been male, as have been most heads of

state, diplomats, and CEOs with disappointingly few excep-
tions. Aristotle, Rousseau, and Freud (just to name a few)
portrayed women as scatterbrained and highly emotional
creatures who lacked logic and reason, and needed to subordinate their minds and their desires to those of men. Over
the centuries, women were told to "bite your tongue," and
when they didn't, punishment was severe; for example, in
Colonial America any woman who was perceived to be a gossip was punished in the town square and made to wear a
"scold's bridle" that would pierce the tongue when she spoke.

Young women who argue that all the battles have been
won tend to think that this sort of thing would never happen
today. They need to think again. When law professor Anita
Hill testified during the Senate hearings regarding Supreme
Court nominee Clarence Thomas, she was vilified in the
press and her personal credibility and emotional integrity
were questioned. Taking an unpopular position, questioning
authority, and speaking against a position held by someone
in the predominantly male establishment remains a risky
business for women.

Each chapter contains stimulating ideas to motivate you to
develop your presentation and public speaking skills. We
encourage you to keep a pad nearby so you can answer some
of the questions we raise in each chapter as you read this book.

Standing up in front of a group and telling folks what
they should think, do, and feel is not something women are
encouraged to do. Nevertheless, a number of women leaders
have learned how to become effective speakers in order to
exert influence and persuade people to adopt a new social or
economic policy, reorganize business operations, and
improve life in their communities. To learn more about their
success as speakers, we interviewed twenty women who regularly speak to groups and the media, often on a national or
international stage.

The women we focus on are appointed or elected officials, executives of advocacy groups, and businesswomen who talked candidly about their personal and work experiences, and their family life. They refer to role models who helped prepare them to be effective speakers. News articles, excerpts of speeches by women leaders (such as Congresswoman Barbara Jordan, Hillary Clinton, Wilma Mankiller, Angela Oh, and Gloria Steinem), and scholarly research are included as references. Women we interviewed also provided excerpts of speeches for inclusion in the book.

In our interviews, we asked women speakers key questions:

- ◆ How did you become confident enough to believe in yourself, your competence, and your message to transcend the very common fear of public speaking?
- ◆ What was it about your early or young adult years that allowed you to become successful leaders and speakers?
- ◆ What strategies do you use to prepare yourself and your material?
- ◆ What minefields have you encountered when you deliver presentations?
- ◆ Do you think that audiences judge women and men differently?
- ◆ How do you know that your presentation was successful?
- ◆ What do you actually enjoy about speaking to groups or audiences?
- ◆ What lessons did you learn from coping with difficult speaking situations?

We address these questions throughout the book. The insights from women speakers that emerge will help you become confident enough to seize—rather than shirk from—future opportunities to be seen and heard.

Finding the courage to speak your mind, speak in public settings, or do both at the same time is a daunting prospect for men as well as for women. Our research, observations, and interviews indicate that while it is particularly difficult for women speakers to be seen and heard as credible leaders, the skills and strategies can be easily learned by motivated individuals. You *can* change your attitude and your audience's, too. We have learned, through trial and error and from good role models, how to speak to groups in ways that enhanced our careers and helped our organizations. We have had the satisfaction of knowing that we made a positive impact on our listeners. We want **you** to have the same satisfaction that comes from being seen, heard, and respected as a leader!

For change to happen, not only do male leaders need to hear from articulate women, but, also, more articulate women need to become leaders. Be assured that you will not be the first to pioneer in uncharted territory. Throughout the book, beginning with **Chapter 2**, you will gain an overview of why public speaking is a particularly dangerous act for women. For men, speaking to groups and audiences is a logical extension of the male role. They assume that people are interested in what they have to say, while women are more tentative. One woman who had been promoted into an executive position in the military wanted to know, "How do I become a commanding presence?" We'll share a range of ideas that will help you develop your own style and confidence in your public voice.

Journalist Barbara Ehrenreich believes that most people are so terrified that they would rather be in the casket than standing next to it and talking to the mourners, but when you have a strategy for addressing problems in the workplace or your community, you'll be tempted to master your fears and speak up in spite of them. Our research does indicate that public speaking has unique traps and minefields for women that make it harder to be seen as credible leaders because audiences do view male and female speakers differently. The act of public speaking is one that we expect men to play by dint of their assigned sex role, and this holds true in most cultures. Denying that these different expectations exist is naive. Understanding that audiences may be skeptical about your capacity to be a leader helps women to develop a more strategic approach to planning their presentations than men need to do.

In **Chapter 3,** we provide you with many of the "lessons learned" by women speakers who have faced and identified the traps and minefields. Their experiences and ideas provide a fresh take on an age-old problem—overcoming the fears surrounding public speaking. Their assistance will help you take your rightful place alongside other leaders, whether in your neighborhood, workplace, in the media, or in your state and national capitols.

The examples and anecdotes from our interviews and from excerpts of speeches by diverse women leaders will inspire you, provide guidance, and demystify the preparation and delivery process. Role models are great because they can encourage each of us to think differently about the mere idea of women as speakers; however, it is not our intention to force you into a particular mold. We'd rather have you say, "If she can do it, so can I!"

"Feminine virtues" are devalued when men are in charge. Some would say that silence is golden when men do all the talking. It's time to topple those old assumptions about women's place in history as we step up to the podium to be seen and heard as leaders. **Chapter 4** addresses the value of a feminine perspective in cultivating speaker skills. Historically, women's feminine traits have been derided; however, we believe that many feminine traits will increase your effectiveness as a speaker. Your ability to read cues, your desire to relate, willingness to share personal anecdotes, express feelings—these can all become the ingredients of a memorable presentation.

Chapter 5 emphasizes your authenticity. You are the unique ingredient in this yeasty speaker development process. Presenting yourself as honestly as you can is as important as presenting your message clearly and directly. Be who you are. The power of being there is the very essence of power, according to a successful speaker. And when you're feeling very alive and aware of the environment—the faces, the excitement the room—you'll be less anxious about what will happen in the future. The individual who knows herself and her 'hot buttons' is less likely to allow someone else to push them during the Q and A. You may not be a CEO, Olympic athlete, or elder statesman, but being authentic enhances your charisma, which, in turn, adds to your credibility as a potential leader.

Chapter 6 discusses the value of your daily life influences that helped shape your ability to present yourself as a "real" person. Girls and young women can develop into self-confident communicators when their sisters, parents, mentors, and role models make them feel important. "Speak up! Your ideas are worth sharing with others" is a critical message, but how many of us were encouraged to do so in those early years? Interviews with speakers reveal several patterns that help younger women develop self-confidence at the podium.

Put your best foot forward instead of in your mouth, and focus on your strengths as a person and a potential leader. **Chapter 7** will provide some tactics and strategies for focusing on your main point that will help you gain credibility as the voice of authority. As a woman speaker, you are like

Ginger Rogers dancing with Fred Astaire; as the joke goes, sure, you both do the same steps, but you have to dance backwards and in high heels. Like men, you have to be organized, prepared, relate to your audience, and convince them that you are leadership material even without gray sideburns, but you don't sound like a leader . . . yet.

How do you shift from the more personal, subjective approach that is typical of novice speakers to a more strategic approach? What strategies can you present to help listeners succeed? What do you have in common? Whether it's a small or a large group of listeners, you'll want to think about the end result and the strategies to get you there. Good conversations may meander; good presentations must be laser-like in their focus. You are the best person to make the case and lead the change. After all, aren't you usually compelled to speak up or get involved because no one else is stepping forward to provide your unique perspective? If you don't, who will?

In **Chapter 8** we make it clear: the road to flawless delivery and power at the podium begins with preparation and practice. No formula, no magic bullet is required to build self-confidence. It's up to you. Relaxation is a state of mind. So is going with the adrenaline rush that comes from facing a group and knowing you're ready for whatever happens. The audience wants you to succeed because if you don't they feel they've wasted their time. Betsy Myers warms up the way athletes do. She gives smaller presentations, appears on panels, watches other speakers, and begins to mentally relax about the upcoming event.

Susan Lowell Butler says that you need to decide if you really want to be there. If you're miserable, and you hate them, it will show, so why bother to pretend that you're relaxed and happy? Once you figure out a way to make contact with the audience, you'll start the adrenaline working to ignite your energy in a positive way.

Want to personalize your presentations in meaningful ways? Remember your own best stories. History confirms that storytelling with a specific purpose is a proven method of being memorable. Former California Superintendent of Public Instruction Delaine Eastin's family prepared her with great material by reminiscing about aunts and uncles' behavior in the good old days. CEO Laura Groppe tells why she's inspired by her favorite poet, Maya Angelou. Women use self-disclosure through storytelling to create intimacy and landscape common ground. When self-disclosure doesn't deteriorate into self-deprecation, which women tend towards, it helps your listeners to trust you. We know that establishing a trusting relationship with your listeners is critical as part of your strategy to gain credibility as a leader. Read more about storytelling strategies in **Chapter 9.**

Building bridges with your audience is one of your first tasks if you are from a different racial, cultural, or ethnic group, and doubly challenging if the audience is primarily male. **Chapter 10** addresses the challenges and opportunities when the speaker is a woman of color.[*] Business leaders like Daisy Exposito believe that diversity provides new opportunities to think differently, as it is "the driving force in shaping today's America." When the speaker is a woman of color, she can discuss local, regional, and national problems—and the consequences of not solving a problem—using personal experiences, anecdotal material, and cultural examples that transcend those cold statistics and might otherwise be ignored by male decision-makers. We believe that she can add a fresh, new voice to analyses of complex social, economic, educational, and political problems that affect everyone.

[*] Note: An earlier version of Chapter 10 was published as "Why Women of Color Need to Speak Up" in the August 2002 *Women's Policy Journal* at the John F. Kennedy School of Government, Harvard University.

The focus in **Chapter 11** is on being more of a strategist when you are presenting yourself as the voice of authority. No need to wait until you've earned the Nobel Prize. Emphasize the expertise gained from personal, professional, or community-building experiences. Your way of "knowing" goes beyond the academic text or conventional credentials, though many audiences do require them before handing you a mike.

We've gained expertise from playing and creatively juggling many (often conflicting) roles that will be worth sharing with others. Women today are challenging the infamous biological clock and listeners will appreciate what a woman has learned, for example, about the unexpected minefields to consider before beginning in-vitro fertilization. You can compare the delights as well as the dangers of traveling alone as a single woman, with slides of you climbing up onto the camel. You can demonstrate how you found the cancerous lump that could otherwise have killed you. Whether saving for retirement in a down market or surviving life as a member of "the sandwich generation"—you have a new spin to put on topics of current interest to men and women today. Whatever you've learned is going to be worth sharing.

Once you begin to use your vocal authority you will be seen as the expert! It may be time to take the show on the road and get paid for your presentations. Preparing yourself to become a paid professional speaker is addressed in **Chapter 12**, the last chapter of our book. While you might not see a professional speaking career in your future right now . . . read on! You'll soon see that it's not out of the question.

It's hard for most women to increase their fees for services rendered, much less charge for their presentations, even when they have developed extensive resumes. We present you with ideas for how to package yourself, and how to expand your networks of potential clients. If this doesn't appeal to you, what about becoming a fulltime spokesperson for your favorite charity? What a bonus it would be if large numbers of people sought you out, wanted to hear you, believed in you, took your advice, and paid you for your words!

You might be wondering how to get started: Which professional associations can help me market my services? How do I find a peer network? What trade journals should I buy? How do I use the media? What are the ingredients of a press kit? When you finish this chapter, you'll know the answers to these and other questions to help you develop a career as a paid professional speaker.

In general, you will be covering a lot of territory as you read this book. Use our questions to guide you in reflecting on your early years, communications skills and abilities, and issues you believe in. Clarify your own positions on issues that you care about. When you're watching television or attending meetings, make mental notes about the speaker's style and delivery. Find new role models—younger, older, women of color—who will demonstrate presentation techniques with which you can experiment. Start a "speakers support group," using this book as the basis of a self-directed workshop for your peers, colleagues, and friends. Life is the best laboratory for continuous learning.

Our reward as authors will be to know that you feel more confident and competent as you speak out on all manner of topics, perceived by your listeners as a credible leader. When you are seen and heard speaking with passionate conviction, your voice will empower others, thereby improving the quality of the debates and discussions about the critical issues that matter most.

CHAPTER 2

Women Speakers Face Unique Challenges

When a woman is placed in a position in which being assertive and forceful is necessary, she is faced with a paradox: she can be a good woman but bad executive or professional; or vice versa. To do both is impossible. As long as a woman stays in 'her place,' at home and in private, the contradiction does not surface.
—Robin Tolmach Lakoff,
Professor of Linguistics[1]

Public speaking is difficult for everyone. In fact, *The Book of Lists* indicates that fear of public speaking is the number one fear of Americans who were surveyed, greater than the fear of death, which is number three.[2] Journalist Sheila Murphy wrote,

"Most people would rather be in the casket than standing next to it and talking to the mourners."[3]

Sociologist Barbara Ehrenreich writes:

At first, I was terrified, and experienced the symptoms—tachycardia, syncope, diarrhea, diuresis, drenching perspiration—so familiar to public speakers and those undergoing heroin detox treatment. In time, however, the symptoms subsided to mere dread and I began

to look forward to speaking occasions in much the same
spirit I approach an amputation or a chance to sample
human flesh.[4]

As we listen to the thunder of our hearts beating, we
wonder: *will I survive?* Ehrenreich calls it "public freaking,"
and that's because we know that the risks are higher than they
are in a private conversation when we can always say later,
"Oh, that's not really what I meant, or thought I said."
Whoever stands up to face a group and express an opinion is
putting her future on the line. In public speaking situations,
there are witnesses, and perhaps even videotape. The speaker
could say something stupid, forget her main point, or inad-
vertently offend someone. She may have her expertise dis-
puted or become the subject of gossip or mockery. Her
motives may be questioned. She may become socially iso-
lated, something women don't particularly enjoy. The
speaker could lose an election or her job and, in turn, her
ability to pay for rent or food. If she is the sole or primary
breadwinner, no wonder that she is reticent about taking the
risks of expressing her ideas in public.

Your intelligence and level of education have little to do
with the anxiety surrounding the speaker role. Heather
Barnett, doctoral student in the psychology program at
Harvard, was petrified about public speaking. Before she had
to speak, her heart would race; she'd get short of breath and
feel hot and sweaty. She went to a behavioral therapist who
advised her to talk early in her classes without waiting to be
called on in order to avoid her fears about not being brilliant
enough when she did speak up. In an interview she disclosed:

. . . I also started taking antianxiety medication . . . .
Later, when I had to lead seminars, I'd rehearse at the
podium in an empty room. That was hugely helpful.
I've [since] discovered that I actually like lecturing, far

more than research . . . . I've found my calling, but I had
to do some intense work on myself to embrace it.[5]

Whenever a person behaves in a way that defies social expectations, anxiety increases. When men speak up, they are comfortable in the role of "speaker," though they may still have fears about public speaking. A woman speaker not only has to manage the physiological anxiety of public speaking that is common to both men and women, but has to manage the anxiety surrounding the role conflict as well. After all, if we're too feminine, how can we be leaders? If we're too masculine, we aren't "normal" women.

In women's case, fear of public speaking might be related to the "imposter syndrome" that is common to women, the belief that one is insufficient and unable to be proficient at an activity that an individual wants or needs to do. These feelings persist even when all information that she receives indicate that the opposite is true.[6] Have you ever felt like an imposter?

Women who are lacking confidence as leaders may feel particularly vulnerable when they are at the front of the room wearing the mantle of leadership, feeling as if they are playing a new role that they were ill-prepared to play. For all these reasons, public speaking is more challenging for women than for men.

Being Taken Seriously at the Podium Is Women's Unique Challenge

Historically, our society hasn't been receptive to women being leaders. Professor Kathleen Hall Jamieson writes that, "Women who speak out are immodest and must be shamed, but women who are silent will be ignored and dismissed."[7] Women speakers are caught in this double bind. Those who speak and behave assertively can be seen as too masculine. These so-called 'masculine' women are often described as "having an edge." However, if speakers are ambiguous, indirect, and don't commit to having strong beliefs, they may be seen as too feminine, too soft, and they certainly aren't going to be taken seriously as leaders. It's a clear case of "damned if you do, damned if you don't." Public speaking is a role conflict for women—one that women leaders must resolve in order to break out of a double bind situtation.

Women can't leave it to men to solve the world's—and their—problems as they did centuries ago when men's role required them to be the protector. Women today must speak for themselves, expressing their unique ideas and opinions, but also speak on behalf of women who have no voice in that particular forum. If women don't present a woman's point of view in debating a new business policy, social policy, or legislative action, who will?[8]

As is now clear, one of the speaker's main tasks is to overcome any negative stereotypes that might linger in the mind of the audience about a woman's capacity to be a leader. Traditional audiences—and, let's not kid ourselves, that means most audiences—believe that a man is a stronger individual by virtue of his sex. A man's powers of persuasion supposedly emanate from his "innate" intelligence, logical and systematic mind, emotional detachment and neutrality, and his ability to focus on one thing at a time. A woman's powers of persuasion, however, are seen as supposedly emanating from her "innate" tendency to be emotional, selfless, seductive, manipulative, coy, and focused on the sanctity of family virtues. Based on these narrow beliefs, whom would you rather vote for? Work for? These destructive stereotypes create enormous obstacles to be overcome by women who wish to be seen and heard as credible leaders.

When they do speak up, even with the necessary and indisputable experience behind them to qualify for state and national leadership positions, women are still judged harshly. Massachusetts' gubernatorial candidate Shannon O'Brien was coached to become aggressive in her debates with Milt Romney, who did go on to win the election; Romney called her behavior "unbecoming" and, ultimately, so did the voters.[9]

It's tough to get good coverage. The media tends to trivialize women's remarks and focus on how they look rather than what they say or how they think about important issues of the day. An article about the possibility of a woman president, which presented an array of possible candidates such as Senators Elizabeth Dole or Hillary Clinton, described the difficulties of getting the right kind of media coverage. No matter how much they emphasized their positions on the issues, the media continued to focus on the three H's: husbands, hairdos, and headbands.[10]

Even today, in our more liberated society, press coverage of women is minimal; only about 25 percent of front-page articles refer to women. Stories about women speakers continue to trivialize the intellectual content of the speech, focusing instead on the speaker's marital status or physical appearance. Advertisements continue to use mainly male voices to sell the big-ticket products, with the exception of those related to cleansers, cosmetics, and fashions.[11]

Leaders must speak effectively to various public audiences and do well in the public communication role. However, the act of public speaking—including public debate—is a challenging role that audiences expect men to play. Even when women defy social conventions and speak as leaders—with appropriate experience and professional credentials, critics are harsh. Consider what happened to Geraldine Ferraro when she ran for vice president in 1984.

Knowing she would be only a heartbeat away from the presidency, the public and the press scrutinized her behavior meticulously. In a public debate with George Bush, however, she performed superbly: she was firm and clear, kept her cool, and was informed, lucid, and direct. Bush behaved much more as what we describe as the hysterical lady: "his voice rose in indignation in both pitch and volume."[12]

He repeated himself and didn't listen; his face got red, and his voice became shrill. After their debate, guess how the media portrayed the debate? The pollsters declared Bush the winner, although not for any particular reason, except that Bush was a man and men are presidents.

Given the advances of women over the past fifteen years, if this debate were to be repeated again today, do you really think that Ferraro would win? Has society really progressed to the point where the public is ready to accept a competent woman in the White House?

Transcending the Limitations of the Feminine Sex Role

When you stand up and face a group or audience, you probably don't want to believe that you are taking a risk based on "masculine" or "feminine" gender stereotypes that have defined women's place for centuries. After all, you're interested in advancement, or you wouldn't be reading this book. Please remember that these stereotypes are so deeply ingrained in the human consciousness that people are usually unaware of their impact but, nonetheless, perceptions do act as a critical filter for how people perceive reality and evaluate what they see and hear.

Conventional sex roles require women to be modest. Speaking up to take a position on an issue can appear to be self-aggrandizing for a woman because we don't expect women to take positions on issues, while it is quite the opposite for men. The double standard for women can be seen in our choice of words describing men and women. After all, it remains the conventional view that unmarried men are *bachelors* but, alas, women who don't marry are *spinsters*.

The same sexist language we commonly use in distinguishing a businessman from a businesswoman may well affect how audiences interpret the speaker's behavior and style:

◆ *A businessman is appropriately aggressive, but a businesswoman is pushy.*

◆ *He follows through, but she doesn't know when to quit.*

◆ *He's firm, but she's stubborn.*

◆ *He's a man of the world, but she's been around.*

◆ *He maintains tough standards, but she's never satisfied.*

◆ *He exercises authority, but she's a tyrant.*

◆ *He's discreet, but she's secretive.*

◆ *He's a stern taskmaster, but she's difficult to work for.*

◆ *He's emotionally sensitive, but she's overly emotional.*

◆ *He's reflective, but she's indecisive.*

If a male speaker has little time to prepare and gives a bad presentation, we say he's *having an off day*, but in similar circumstances she was *scatterbrained* and . . . what did we expect anyway? All of the ways in which we stereotype women if they deviate from the conventional role reflect a double-standard—one that makes both women and men in an audience more critical of women when they speak, even when the speaker is graced with intelligence, credentials, and expertise.

Sociologists and psychologists have observed the very early manifestations of sex roles in young children, particularly in terms of communication style in ways that prepare boys to become public people. For example:

- ◆ Boys are more physically active, play in teams, and are used to audiences, crowds and being observed, cheered on, and applauded.

- ◆ Boys in general, are more verbally aggressive; they brag, use commands, boast, and use their authority.

- ◆ Boys will heckle a speaker, and insult their opponents.

- ◆ Boys influence their peers by making direct demands.

- ◆ Boys stay on topic.

- ◆ Boys interrupt girls, seizing the topic of conversation when they converse together.

- ◆ Girls are less physically active than boys, play with one another and more typically with one friend or in small groups.

- ◆ Girls, in general, are less verbally aggressive; they don't brag, use direct commands, boast about their accomplishments, or use their authority.

- ◆ Girls don't heckle a speaker or insult their opponents, at least not in public ways.

- ◆ Girls attempt to influence their peers through polite suggestions and, if there are disagreements, they aren't handled directly.

- ◆ Girls talk off-topic, and interrupt one another.

- ◆ Girls allow boys to interrupt them and to seize control of the conversation when they converse together.[13]

All of these early socializing influences contribute to women's reticence and inhibitions about speaking up in groups, influencing other people through argument, or asserting their authority, whether real authority or their ability to use their personal charisma to influence others. While younger women might argue that, "things are changing," gender research has not negated conventional communication patterns evident in our society.

Of course, both women and men have the capacity for intelligence and creativity. In fact, women have better verbal skills, though they tend to excel in interpersonal conversations and small groups, rather than public speaking situations. Women have been thought to have greater insight about themselves and tend to disclose personal problems and difficulties in a self-effacing manner; men tend to keep up a façade and disclose fewer personal problems. Women are typically more social and empathetic than men are.

Given the fact that society values male traits and devalues female traits, strategy is critical. The woman speaker's job at the podium is not merely to plan and deliver her message effectively, but to realize that her "meta- message," if you will, is: "**I am a capable leader.**" If the audience doesn't believe her, all the time spent on organizing and preparing her ideas will be wasted. The audience is sizing her up, wondering about her ability to wield power and influence in a leadership role:

* *Does she have access to resources and networks?*
* *Can she handle conflicts and tough negotiations?*
* *Will she be manipulated by her feelings more easily than a man would be?*
* *Will she keep her eye on the big picture or get lost in the details?*

- *Was her previous success due to a round of good luck or does she have what it takes to be a leader?*
- *Is she in for the long haul or will she retreat to home and hearth when her biological clock goes off?*
- *Does she look like a leader? Does she sound like a leader?*

It is only after the listeners feel confident that the speaker has leadership skills that they will pay attention to the content of her presentation. If a leader is imagined to be a tall man with gray sideburns, probably that's not you. So what does a woman leader look like? We're new at this game, which means that we can experiment with dress. However, no matter the circumstance, a leader doesn't sound like a young girl. What a woman might not possess in terms of the conventional "image" of a leader, she can make up for in using her voice forcefully to convey a commanding presence.

Audiences are also evaluating the speaker's attractiveness—whether she is "attractive" in a conventional way. It wouldn't be hard to fail since the standard of attractiveness—for women—blonde, white, and bone thin—was defined by film or network television or our youth-oriented MTV culture. Is the speaker a nice person who smiles easily? Does she seem flexible? Is she married? In other words, is she a "normal" woman? Achieving femininity in conventional terms is the key to acceptance for many listeners. Realize that if you are too far afield from your audience in terms of their standard of "conventional" attractiveness, you are taking a risk, although we are not advising you against doing so. Do consider whether this is the time for a corporate pantsuit, bell-bottoms, or a dress. Your image is part of your strategy in being seen and heard as a leader.

Overcoming a Tentative Style

Historically, men have been in charge of making observable changes in the real world of everyday commerce, as well as in the more ephemeral world through organized religion. Therefore, men's language is the language of the powerful. They are less likely to worry about being offensive to their listeners. In the past, women have not been in charge of resources such as capital and real estate, nor have they had political strength or legal protection equal to men's. Men have relegated interpersonal matters to women: caring for others, being responsive to practical matters, and handling the everyday particulars of domestic life.

By contrast, women have survived in society through their skills at listening, agreeing more than confronting, and being indirect. Women had only been able to express radical ideas when the authority figures were out of range, rather than direct confrontation, out of fear of repercussions, which was probably wise. As a result of the real risks of speaking up in certain situations and under some conditions over the centuries, women's language has generally developed an indirect and more tentative style. This style may well inhibit their ability to be taken seriously by audiences.

Research about women's language informs us about the following tendencies:

◆ Women make more use of expressive forms such as empty adjectives (e.g. "fabulous!" "nice," "lovely," or "divine") and emotional evaluations (e.g., "I hated it!" "I loved it!").

◆ Women use forms that convey a lack of precision, such as "so" or "such," rather than quantifying amounts of time, space, weight, numbers, and percentages.

◆ Women use hedges of all kinds ("I'm not sure") and qualifiers ("sort of" or "kind of") more than men do.

◆ Women tend to relate what others think before they convey what they think or their position.[14]

An analysis of body language found that submissive behaviors were more typical of females and subordinates. These include lowering or averting the eyes, blinking, smiling, and an expressive face. The feminine posture is tighter with legs held together and arms held close to the body. Gestures range from small and inhibited to excessive in some cultures. Women's intonation is higher pitched (which can be seen as more emotional or even hysterical). Women don't initiate touch but yield to being touched. Women maintain a small envelope of space. Until recently, clothing worn by women tended to be constraining or form-fitting in ways that made it difficult to move around comfortably or gesture broadly. Women's speaking habits allow for interruptions and the topic to be changed or redirected by the other party, particularly when men are "the other party." In male-female conversation, women tend to talk less often and for less time and ask questions as opposed to making statements.[15]

A feminine voice is breathier. The voice may be thinner and less robust. A throaty voice in men indicates a more sophisticated or well-adjusted personality type but in women indicates a less intelligent persona, a more boorish, neurotic or quiet personality type.[16] Women use intonation patterns that turn their statements into questions; for example, try saying the following sentence with an upward and then a downward inflection at the end: "My report is not quite complete." You can convey confidence in your point through your voice more than your words.

Men expect women's talk to be trivial and to focus on domestic matters and stories about other people without facts to back them up. If you want to be taken seriously as a leader, you must become more aware of your tendencies to speak in ways that weaken your credibility as a leader. You want to convey to the listeners that you, as a leader, have a clear, rational mind as well as a heart.

Each woman has to be aware of her verbal and nonverbal speech tendencies and adjust them to meet the challenges of the public speaking situation. Do you sound like a leader? You may want to conduct an experiment. Audiotape yourself in a conversation with a colleague or friend about an issue or a problem. *Was your language clear? If not, what made it difficult to follow your key points? Did you assert your opinion clearly? Was your voice breathy or did you speak from your diaphragm in a deeper voice, conveying maturity and confidence?*

Videotape yourself giving a presentation to a group or an audience. *Did you look like a leader? Notice the degree to which you gesture and make eye contact. Did your manner of dress confine you to small gestures or inhibit you from being assertive and forceful?* Just as your style of speaking, body language, and voice are learned behaviors, they can be unlearned if you need to do so to strengthen your style. Making necessary changes in your speech, language, and style to transcend negative stereotypes is a critical strategy, if you want to be seen and heard as a leader.

LESSON
*Public speaking presents unique challenges
for women because it remains unusual to see women
in top leadership positions and at the podium
or microphone.*

Section Two

PRIVATE VOICE, PUBLIC VOICE

CHAPTER 3

Role Models

This was the ultimate table, and I realized that no woman had ever sat at that table before in the history of our country, ... And I swear to you that for a moment I felt the spirit of Susan B. Anthony in the room with me.[17]
—Congresswoman Nancy Pelosi
first female Democratic Leader
of the House of Representatives

Successful women speakers are individuals who believe in themselves and the wisdom that comes from their role models as well as the knowledge gained from playing many roles in life. When contemporary women leaders have something important to say, they are determined to be seen, heard, and taken seriously. In asserting their ideas and opinions in public, these speakers are willing to take whatever risks are involved. If they had any reticence or personal conflicts about the speaker role, these feelings are overshadowed by a need to communicate their message to a particular group or audience. They realize that if they don't speak up to express a point of view or call for action, it's possible that no one else will take the lead on a particular issue.

For the purposes of learning from contemporary role models, we interviewed women who are advocates, elected and appointed leaders, or administrators who must speak to groups or audiences by dint of their roles (See biographical list in Appendix.) They had their "favorite" speakers who are role models for them, and we've excerpted quotes from speakers they—and we—admire. Dynamic women leaders are role models for the rest of us because they demonstrate high standards of excellence in the way that they exert leadership and influence through their speeches and presentations. Specifically, successful women speakers demonstrate intelligence, competence, assertiveness, and an ability to think on their feet. They relate to their audiences in professional ways that also include being personal, sharing anecdotes, and a willingness to express feelings, as appropriate. They know their audiences' needs and direct their remarks so as to fit these needs. They read nonverbal cues well and can switch gears when the situation allows them to do so.

Analyze the speaking skills of increasing numbers of emerging and established women leaders by watching them deliver presentations on CNN on any given day. Thanks to a multi-media global telecommunications system, we have improved access to multi-cultural and multi-racial role models who demonstrate different speaking styles. These modern day role models demonstrate how women might present their ideas more effectively.

Learning through observation is important if you are the first woman in a particular role, whether as manager or the first woman mayor, the first woman astronaut, the first female ".com" CEO, the first female senator from your state, or the first female college president. If you are the first woman "anything," your performance will be scrutinized by the establishment and compared to your male predecessors in that role, and that includes your performance as a speaker. If, on the other hand, you take some risks and succeed as an

articulate and eloquent leader, you will be admired and emu-
lated by other women who realize they can follow in your
footsteps.

Justice Sandra Day O'Connor talked about how excited
she was when Ruth Bader Ginsburg—the second woman—
was named to the U.S. Supreme Court. She said that only
then was she able to be a Justice. "When you're the only anything, it's a different set of dynamics, a different set of challenges."[18]

If she is "the first," audiences will certainly be wondering
about her competence and expertise. As a woman speaker,
she has a smaller margin of error than a man would have.
The proving ground starts at the podium.

We do have increasing numbers of women who are contemporary role models. If you asked a group of working
women to come up with a list of intelligent, articulate, and
accomplished speakers during the past twenty years, it would
probably include Gloria Steinem. Journalist, outspoken feminist, and publisher of *Ms.* magazine, she is well organized
and conversational in her style. She was described by an associate as a great speaker who can take on difficult people
during a Q and A session in a powerful way. Ann Richards,
former governor of Texas, is known for her plain speaking
and firecracker wit, storytelling skills, and Texas homilies.
Senator Elizabeth Dole has a warm and folksy style when she
needs to and has been known to work the room in Oprah
style during her presentations.

Senator and former First Lady Hillary Clinton is known
as a brilliant strategist who is philosophical, can think on her
feet, and has a great capacity for recalling facts and dates. She
has had to learn how to cope with the media frenzy accompanying her husband's infidelity while being in the public eye
in her own right. While she ran for the Senate, viewers saw

her maintaining her composure during difficult interviews that focused on private matters and ignored policy issues.

Many women of color deal with controversial issues and are outstanding speakers. Attorney Angela Oh, who was an appointee to Clinton's Commission on Race, is straightforward in her style. Wilma Mankiller, chief of the Cherokee nation is informal and conversational, using a storytelling style when appropriate. Dolores Huerta, president of the United Farmworkers Union, walks the talk when she marches with the farmworkers after she speaks. Anita Hill, Professor of Law and Women's Studies at Brandeis University, has a quiet voice and thoughtful style that conveys sincerity and honesty. These women have found that their stories hold up well and bear repeating.

There are many outstanding Black women speakers who are role models for all women. One of the most outstanding speakers of the twentieth century was the late Barbara Jordan, a Black congresswoman from Texas who was lauded for her eloquent speech style and leadership during the Watergate hearings. During the hearings, she said, " It is reason and not passion which must guide our deliberations, guide our debate, and guide our decision."[19] In terms of her sonorous voice and dramatic delivery style, Jordan raised the bar very high for the rest of us.

Alexis Herman, former secretary of labor, has a more formal style as was appropriate to her position but also used self-disclosure—even in formal settings—when appropriate to inspire groups to work together. Betsy Myers, former director of the White House Office of Women believes that Herman displays "unbelievable class and dignity." In an interview, Ida Castro, former director of The Equal Employment Opportunities Commission and The Women's Bureau describes Herman's delivery as "a total involvement with her message, a commitment to what she is saying, a belief in what she says, and a delivery that is flawless."

Harvard Law Professor Lani Guinier combines personal anecdotes, academic research, and legal references to make her points in a memorable manner. Spelman College President Jeanetta Cole can tell the same favorite story over and over again—telling it long, short, or in a new way. Sociologist Barbara Ehrenreich wrote about the people she admires, "women like civil rights activist Fannie Lou Hammer, who . . . are out there raising hell, changing the landscape for women and for everyone."[20]

Barbara Lee, a Black congresswoman from northern California, was the sole lawmaker to vote against using force in response to the September 11 terrorist attacks on the United States and has a forceful style when she needs to assert her authority.

The women speakers listed above are smart and strong individuals. Not one of them is like any other. Their expertise comes not only from academic learning but also from "the school of hard knocks." They share some common life experiences as women. They can bridge status differentials and communicate across cultures, and yet each speaker's personal style is unique. The charismatic presence of an outstanding speaker is almost palpable; you'd know from the buzz in the air when they're in the room and, by contrast, you'd also immediately sense when they've left.

Why Are Role Models Critical to Women Speakers?

A role model is someone who shows us how to play a role in an exemplary manner, demonstrating how something is done. She sets a standard for others. As a speaker, she has mastered the mental models, techniques, and tools necessary to be effective. This would include her ability to be strategic in preparing herself and her material for a presentation. She recognizes that she must know her material, organize her ideas and handouts, be able to relate to the audience, prepare memorable quotes and sound bites in advance, predict the tough questions, and manage her image and appearance. She rehearses her presentation in advance to respect the time constraints. If she wanted publicity, she would develop a press kit to attract the media to her presentation. She'd prepare alliterative quotes or a "spin" that would appeal to the press who will otherwise construct their own sound bites in the absence of hers. This is a complex constellation of tasks.

When we watch role models in action, they make public speaking look easy, and we think, "Hmmmm. I can do that." When Lois is stuck, she imagines, "How would Hillary answer a tough question?" Anita wonders, "How would Alexis Herman deal with a difficult person?" Whomever you select as positive role models, notice how they work the audience to take charge of the situation. As people who deliver many presentations and speeches on a regular basis, we have identified several role models whom we admire, and we encourage you to do the same.

Whom do outstanding speakers identify as *their* role models? Hillary Clinton often speaks about how Eleanor Roosevelt has been a role model for her. First Lady Eleanor Roosevelt was a self-effacing young woman who was terribly shy. She could easily have lived in her husband's shadow but found the courage of her convictions transformational. When she spoke out for racial justice on an international stage, she was confident that this was the right thing to do. Interestingly, both women experienced anguish in their private lives because of their husbands' infidelity. Nevertheless, they moved forward with their political agendas and spoke for themselves on a range of social issues. In 1995, Hillary spoke at the dedication of Eleanor Roosevelt College. The focal point of her remarks was choice:

> *Eleanor Roosevelt understood that every one of us every day has choices to make about the kind of person we are and what we wish to become. You can decide to be someone who brings people together, or you can fall prey to those who wish to divide us. You can be someone who educates yourself, or you can believe that being negative is clever and being cynical is fashionable. You have a choice.*[21]

Former CEO of AAUW Janice Weinman finds a role model in Marian Wright Edelman, attorney and advocate for children, who speaks out of her own convictions with riveting stories and examples to grab the listener's heart and mind. Edelman's speeches inspire people to give of themselves. As she said at Howard University:

> *Service is the rent we pay for being. It is the very purpose of life, and not something you do in your spare time.*[22]

Role models make us appreciate the importance of the speaker's choice of words that are used to make a point. Short and sweet, Edelman reframes the notion of community service in a democratic society as something that everyone must do.

Good Speakers Inspire Others to Step Up to the Podium

Liz Carpenter, seasoned political pro, has seen many women speakers come and go. In comparing the effectiveness of different styles, she was emphatic:

> *As far as wonderful women speakers, Barbara Jordan was incredible. Her style, however, was more like a performance . . . you never had much real contact with Barbara Jordan, but her power as a speaker is unsurpassed.*

Jordan's testimony at the Whitewater hearings included a powerful call to action to preserve democratic principles. Her eloquence has been analyzed and memorialized, and her speeches are available to the public on the "Gifts of Speech" website.[23]

Most speakers we interviewed mentioned Hillary Clinton as an incredible speaker. Carpenter remarks, "When she's with a group of women in a friendly setting she's tremendous in a different way because her mind is encyclopedic and her ability to command facts and figures makes her an outstanding communicator." Betsy Myers has seen Hillary speak often in formal and informal occasions and is impressed that "she can get up right out of the box and still is so brilliant, including her knowledge of the facts as well as her experiences." When Hillary spoke at the Women.Future satellite conference[24] that involved women business leaders and professional women from Silicon Valley to Silicon Alley committed to creating positive global change by transforming the world of work, the rhetoric tripped off her tongue, and she used impressive stats. Unlike her coached performances on late-night television, the quick wit was all her own.

While major broadcasting companies certainly provide us with women news anchors, CNN has provided new international role models accessible to any woman who watches television. Carpenter likes the fact that they use normal looking people.

> *You used to just see Brooks Brothers suits and a maroon tie and now you see a lot more variety. People today*

want to be like Cokie Roberts, Katie Couric, and Diane Sawyer. We have stood taller because of those women on television.

Ann Richards is known for her sense of humor, acerbic wit, and quotable quotes. In being a keynote speaker at the Democratic Convention in July 1988, she used regionalisms to poke fun at her opponent when she said "that old dog won't hunt. *We're* going to tell how the cow ate the cabbage."[25]

Liz Carpenter knows that people expect her to be funny.

When I'm asked to make a speech, they're asking me because I will amuse them and inspire them. That's what I hope to do [and] I sprinkle my speech with human anecdotes but I don't always want to be funny —that can be really wearing.

Listen and Learn

Consider the example of California Congresswoman Barbara Lee, who was the only member to vote against a House Resolution giving additional powers to President Bush three days after the World Trade Center attack on September 11, 2001. Lee was able to demonstrate tenacity representing her constituents and courage in questioning the wisdom of this decision. She argued that:

Our Constitution provides for checks and balances between our branches of government. This resolution does not obligate the president to report back to Congress after sixty days, as was required by Congress during the Gulf War, about the actions our military will take. Additionally, this resolution authorizes an open-ended action and significantly reduces Congress's authority in this matter. We must bring the perpetrators of this horrific action to justice. But during this

period of grief, mourning, and anger, the U.S. Congress
has a responsibility to urge the use of restraint so that
the violence does not spiral out of control and to con-
sider all of the implications of our actions.[26]

Contradictory to a feminine stereotype, Congresswoman
Lee urged Congress to keep a cool head. You may not agree
with her politics, but she delivered her unpopular position in
a level-headed style.

Watching speakers keep their cool while handling difficult
questions is instructive. Not surprisingly, women crossed
party lines in being more impressed than men by Hillary
Clinton's handling of reporters' questions during the weeks
before and after her husband's impeachment proceedings. In
the Senatorial debate between New York Representative Rick
Lazio and Hillary Clinton prior to his defeat and her election,
she remained cool when asked a loaded question—why she
stayed with her husband—and got back to her main message.

The choices that I've made are right for me. I can't talk
about anybody else's choice. I can only say that mine are
rooted in my religious faith, in my strong sense of fam-
ily, and in what I believe is right and important. I want
to be sure that there's a voice in the Senate that reminds
us that we're still threatened with the right to choose
that might disappear if the wrong person is elected pres-
ident, the wrong people are elected to the Senate. I think
my experience as a woman will make me the kind of
senator who really understands what's at stake.[27]

Given the press' penchant for "dish," celebrity speakers—
and that includes politicians—walk a fine line between self-
disclosure and self-congratulations, and the good speakers
know the difference. Listeners get antsy when the stories are
self-indulgent or self-aggrandizing rather than on point.
Disclosing personal information may or may not be appro-

priate to the topic. Marie Wilson, director of the Ms. Foundation, believes there is a line where talking about your life is appropriate and the right thing to do but "sometimes people use the podium as a way to do their own therapy. There needs to be some guarding against that." Speakers need to realize that they are in a privileged position and abusing that privilege is guaranteed to turn off the audience.

Pay close attention when you hear a woman deviate from her prepared remarks to impulsively share an intimate story with her audience. Did she retain her credibility or cross the line into an overly emotional presentation, thus manifesting the stereotype of a woman who is a victim or an hysteric?

Janice Weinman has watched many outstanding women leaders rise to national recognition because they knew how to integrate emotionality into their presentations, and she has a few favorites:

> *[The late former Congresswoman] Bella Abzug raises consciousness and generates a very strong sense of purpose in the people she is talking to, regardless of their politics and her style. Marian Wright Edelman speaks with very strong personal convictions and out of her own experience. You really feel that what she has to say is a reflection of her own ideology and conviction, rather than a statement of purpose that is abstract from who she is personally.*

Role models show us how to seize and freeze the moment through eloquence. When women such as Geraldine Ferraro and Wilma Mankiller were being inducted into the National Women's Hall of Fame in an old Presbyterian Church in Seneca Falls, New York, keynote speaker Shirley Chisholm rendered her audience breathless with her eloquence. Chisholm, a Black urban leader and former congresswoman from New York, began by saying, "I feel the sisters here. . . . I feel Stanton's power is here with us."[28] Chisholm's decision to identify with the early suffragettes, who were primarily white women, was not lost on the crowd.

You can develop your own style and confidence by observing and learning from dynamic women speakers in action. Outstanding speakers who are our modern-day role models certainly demonstrate how to appropriately incorporate those personal traits that had been denigrated as "feminine" in ways that made them more, not less effective as speakers. After observing role models who know what they're doing, you can experiment through trial and error, modifying some of their techniques and strategies that feel comfortable for you, given your personality. Today's modern women don't want to be carbon copies of men or even other women. We all want choices in every aspect of life, including the choice to develop our own presentation style.

While it is critical that you and I have contemporary role models, Marie Wilson of the Ms. Foundation cautioned against recommending the same formula for everyone.

> *What works for everybody is who they are, and how well that comes through [to the audience]. For example, Ann Richards can stand up and use a very strong accent that is her accent. . . . A Southern accent is often equated with—let's be honest—'you're not smart.' But Ann Richards can use that accent and almost exaggerates it; it's so authentic it becomes part of her power. You have to be careful about thinking there's a single voice, a single language, or any kind of format because, again, it's what works for you.*

What you and I need to find is encouragement to speak up, knowing that delivering effective presentations is a critical strategy for seeking and retaining leadership roles. We need encouragement because the numbers of women at the top of organizations and institutions remain low and the obstacles to success as leaders remain. Women who have ambitious dreams must persist in cultivating these skills, in spite of the double standards and double binds they face in assuming the public speaking role. Tenacious leaders learn to become strategists and prepare for the tough questions from skeptical audiences or hostile reporters. They develop a Teflon capacity to ignore mean spirited questions and, instead, stay focused on their message.

Outstanding speakers speak in a conversational tone. They capitalize on their ability as women to forge relationships and are comfortable relating meaningful anecdotes, sharing personal feelings and disclosing background information, in ways that are appropriate to a public role. Still they remain focused on their particular message, which might be *"Adopt a flex-time policy," "Let's improve our services by being more of a team," "We need a stop sign on the corner,"* or *"Vote for me."*

Women know that communication is a process and that important messages bear repeating. Women get things done through their networks and relationships, and each of these groups and individuals form particular audiences we must cultivate. Then, too, as a woman describing your vision or groundbreaking accomplishments in a public venue or the media, you are a role model for others and will make it easier for the women speakers who come after you. After all, as a pioneer, you are blazing a trail to the podium. There are lessons to be learned from historical and contemporary role models—those women who overcame their fears of public speaking in order to change the world.

LESSON
*We can learn public communication skills
and strategies from new role models.*

CHAPTER 4

Feminine Traits

A recent lawsuit that was twenty-three years in the making determined that the international broadcasting program called "Voice of America" did indeed discriminate against women writers, broadcasters, and technicians. Why? Simply because the employers believed that the "Voice of America" was a male voice. Although the settlement amounted to almost twenty-five million dollars, some would say it was too little too late for the many employees who never lived long enough to see the resolution of the case.[29]

The voice of authority has always been a male voice. Think about it. The voice of the Catholic Church is male. Heads of state and diplomats—with few exceptions—have always been male. The president of the United States: male. CEOs are typically male, even today. As the twenty-first century gets underway, there is still tremendous resistance to associating the female voice with legitimate authority.

When men speak to groups or audiences, the speech is about the message. For women, the speech is about their relationship with the audience. This makes sense. The conventional sex-role socialization experience develops a woman's capacity to empathize with other people and to get things done by working with others and through family, friendship, and collegial networks. Women learn by sharing experiences. They gain power by exchanging information and providing access to one another's networks. These same "feminine" skills can be the basis for her strength as a speaker, particularly in terms of transferring women's listening skills, conversational skills, and reading nonverbal cues to the public communication venue.

Listening skills allow women to more effectively relate to others. Women enjoy listening to others as much as speaking, particularly when they are conversing with friends or co-workers. You've probably heard the expression, "I've got two ears and one mouth, all the better to listen twice as much as I talk." Listening helps the speaker know more about the ground she's standing on—not a bad idea when, for centuries, it wasn't safe for women to challenge authority. Women like to ask, *What's new? What's up? What's hot?* These same questions are helpful to ask prior to your presentation because it gives you, as the speaker, an edge in understanding what's on people's minds so that you can align your topic to common concerns. Then you can communicate that you empathize with the group's predicament and point of view.

After doing some detective work before your presentation, ask yourself: *What new information did I learn that could be incorporated into my presentation?* As a personal example, author Lois Phillips might have said the following if she addressed a board of trustees at their annual planning retreat:

> *In 1969 my mother died of breast cancer because it was poorly diagnosed and treated. My mom would have been alive today if she'd had the benefit of new technologies and treatment options. In spite of the uncertain economy and the fact that you are a new board, you must seize the opportunity to save thousands of women's lives—including the daughters, sisters, and mothers of your friends, family, and colleagues. I have five strategies to jumpstart your five-million-dollar*

clinical trials research campaign, beginning tonight.

Conversational skills are critical. Women enjoy conversations, and the natural propensity for achieving an informal tone creates a sense of confidentiality and intimacy with an audience. In a conversation between two persons, there is an easy flow of ideas and banter, and you aren't sure where the conversation will meander; however, when it's a good conversation, both people are making good contact, getting to know one another, and looking each other in the eye. Expressions like *"Do you believe this?"* and *"Has this ever happened to you?"* or *"Am I crazy, or what?"* can be incorporated into your remarks to create a sense of easy informality and camaraderie.

By contrast, a friend once told a poignant story about a one-way conversation at a dinner party for faculty members and their spouses. This occurred at a time in her life when she was a faculty wife and stay-at-home mom.

> *I listened to my husband's male colleague talk at length about his work. I asked good questions, made connections between the points, and probed deeply about what this all meant. At the end of a rather lengthy conversation and awkward pause, I asked him, 'Well, I guess you're dying to hear the same about me and what I'm up to these days.' To that he replied, 'Well, no, not really.'*

Thud! This is the opposite of how a good conversation can make you feel. You'll want to convey the same warmth, attention, interest in the audience, and informal style in the formal presentation as you would in a conversation, though the presentation is typically constructed to be a monologue. It's not easy to accomplish, but a skilled presenter conveys that "This presentation is about *you*," and "I'm more interested in *you* than in me."

Nonverbal communication skills are essential if a

speaker is going to be successful. Psychological research
shows that women, by and large, are better than men at reading nonverbal cues and at expressing their feelings nonver-
bally.[30] This skill can serve you well. If the audience looks
bored, switch gears rather than barrel on. Maybe it's time to
refer to a humorous anecdote from today's newspaper, or dis-
play a great cartoon from *The New Yorker*. If the audience is
restless, you'll know what to do. Looking out at the audience,
rather than reading from a prepared manuscript will provide
you with ongoing feedback and helps re-establish contact.

The eyes are said to be windows to the soul, but how
many people take the time or the risk to look through that
window? Many speakers get caught up in their message and
barrel forward without making eye contact. Mistake!

Eye contact is an important source of feedback. Have you
ever found yourself fixating on one corner of the room, thus
ignoring everyone else? It could be a manifestation of nervousness or being locked into a manuscript, but when a speaker
avoids eye contact, the audience feels that she isn't really interested in them. If you're not comfortable in person, you might
as well stay home and deliver your remarks via voice mail. To
overcome the tendency to look down at your notes, the floor,
or the air conditioner in the back window, imagine a golden
triangle in the room. Find three friendly faces: one to your left,
one to the right, and one in the center at the back of the room.
Make one point at a time to one person at a time in order to
get yourself rolling. You'll find that you become more relaxed
when you maintain a smaller range of focus. Scanning the
group—or the tops of people's heads—as you speak heightens
anxiety; by contrast, making contact with one person at a time
lessens the chances that you will lose your place as you move
through your remarks. Students and clients swear that this
strategy works well on many levels.

Outstanding women speakers excel at reading nonverbal cues. They check for feedback by interpreting body language. Women speakers notice when listeners look at the ceiling or squint their eyes or shake their heads in disbelief. Are you able to read your audience like a book? Is the listener tilting her head to one side, nodding and smiling? You're on the same page, so to speak. Is the listener sitting with her arms crossed or shaking her head in disagreement? You're not connecting, so try your quote, visual aid, emotional story, or joke to pull her back into 'your story.'

Labor educator Ida Castro believes in watching for signals by the way people react.

You know people are paying attention to you by their body language. The minute you start you can tell whom you have grabbed and whom you haven't touched. You can tell who you need to stare at . . . in order to connect with them.

Maybe it's time for No-More-Ms.-Nice-Gal. Take off the white gloves, and show a few shocking statistics on an overhead slide. Is your audience complacent, apathetic, or in denial about a disastrous problem? Help them to get the big picture by displaying a stunning aerial photograph or a demonstration. Before they hang up, sense that disconnection by reading non-verbal feedback, and then wake them up. Break an egg, shake those jellybeans in the jar, play some music, take a hammer to a statue—whatever it takes. Think back to the last dull presentation you observed: *how did listeners convey disinterest, and what could the speaker have done to re-engage them?*

Ida Castro is accustomed to speaking to male audiences because she was a labor educator whose students were machinists, teamsters, and members of the construction industry. She knew how important it was to immediately grab their attention.

> *I had to develop what I fondly call "the hook." How do*
> *I figure out and express to them in a way that they fig-*
> *ure that the issue [my topic] is critical to them and that*
> *they can't go on one more minute without knowing*
> *this. The light bulb needs to go on and they need to say*
> *"Holy Shit!" I start off by speaking about a number of*
> *issues . . . and see where the lights are in their faces. The*
> *one issue that grabs them is the one that I will develop.*

Her "hook" strategy is based on her appreciation for the value of nonverbal feedback. Are you willing to look your audience in the eye in order to evaluate how well you are doing? If you have the courage to do so, you'll notice if they are fidgety, and you can make immediate adjustments to your pace, vocal variety, and arrangement of material.

Are Women Too Modest?

If feminine socialization means that women have been raised to be modest, then women speakers will think twice about their capabilities and where they have unique and relevant expertise or knowledge. They can more comfortably brag about their staff (or volunteers) instead of their own accomplishments. Being modest can actually work to your advantage, particularly when members of the audience are being applauded.

Women tend to be unassuming and self-disclosing, perhaps to a fault. Modesty, a key feminine virtue, can be appealing to audiences when they realize that a speaker is admitting that she's new at the leadership game, admitting, "I'm human, I'll make mistakes, and I don't know everything, so let's figure this tough problem out together." By contrast, we've all heard speakers who forge on ahead from a prepared text, asserting strong opinions, no matter what the audience's reaction might be. Which leader is worth your trust?

Former Governor Ann Richards has described the years after her divorce with disarming candor and humor. It was a time when, she admits, "I smoked like a chimney and drank like a fish."[31] By being honest, she took control of the situation before anyone else could put a spin on this chapter of her life, and made it clear that all this was behind her. She then went on to discuss her plan of action as a candidate. Now she travels the country speaking about osteoporosis, and again speaks candidly about her family history and her own condition.

Some speakers establish credibility by being proud of what they've accomplished; they know how to walk that fine line between being self-aggrandizing and self-deprecating. Women haven't been encouraged to brag about their accomplishments, so it's unlikely we'll go overboard when we start to do so. Secretary of Labor Alexis Herman is described as having dignity; she brings that confidence in herself to the podium. Shirley Chisholm was a Black congresswoman and presidential candidate who was described as having the charisma that comes from being "very real."[32]

> She ran a day care center and nursery before she went to Congress. . . . When she said it would take two million dollars to provide healthcare, you believed her.[33]

Whether you think you are outstanding or just plan ordinary, you must begin to take yourself seriously as a person who can make things happen. If you want to make the audience believe you're a leader worth listening to, you have to believe in yourself. Start today by listing three accomplishments that give you pride in yourself, and call three friends to share your list.

What about "Womanly Intuition?"

When a man uses his intuition, he's praised for connecting the dots, putting fragmented pieces of information together, or finding structure within chaos. When a woman uses hers, it can be disparaged as, "Oh, it's just womanly intuition." Your sixth sense is a part of your intelligence, a form of radar, allowing you to "read" the crowd. Until the last moments before you begin to speak—and even during your presentation—you can revise your remarks to respond to what you sense is occurring. Your intuition—not a prepared report—helps you to discover the energy of the group at that very moment. Ask yourself: what is the tone of the meeting? Maybe you should learn more about the group's political climate. Is there the possibility of a "hidden agenda" at the conference? Trust your instincts.

Betsy Myers sees woman's intuition as a positive force in being an effective speaker. She trusts her ability to feel out an audience and seeks opportunities to get to know individuals in the room. Although she prepares five major points of the presentation beforehand she remains open to refining her remarks. She allows herself the time to go to lunch with people before her presentation in order to cultivate the relationships with key players or representatives of the group. She will also work the room, trying to intuit:

◆ *Is this an audience that is with me, or not with me?*

◆ *Should I shorten (the talk) or should I lengthen it?*

◆ *Should I tell more stories?*

◆ *What are the hot issues?*

As a result of your radar or sixth sense, you may decide to drop your prepared remarks entirely and open the group up to a question-and-answer format. A skilled presenter will use

the questions from the audience to jump back to her prepared material anyway. Taking a calculated risk is a function
of your intuition; it informs you about what's in your best
interest as a presenter.

Relationship Skills Can Strengthen Your Presentation

As more women seek to move into decision-making roles in
the workplace and their communities, we are learning more
about how they manage and lead people. Research has confirmed that women's leadership style is relational and that
relating to people through ongoing communication is a key
part of their strategy to be effective. Certain skills that are
tied to feminine behavior and attitudes have been found to be
extremely positive in motivating and retaining staff in a wide
variety of settings. Businesswomen are just as interested in
the bottom line as male managers, but their way of achieving
them is different; women consider results in terms of 1) how
results are achieved and 2) how results impact people.
Women know that you can't achieve bottom line results without delivering regular reports to groups, boards, investors
and the press.

How are those "feminine" traits valuable when a woman
works with others? Maintaining high morale along with productivity is easy for someone with those "feminine" relational
skills. Listening to others when you solicit input about the
organization makes your staff and colleagues feel important—a good investment of a manager's time when you think
of how expensive it is to replace loyal employees. People
often leave positions when they feel ignored or out of the
loop, not because they dislike their jobs. Effective women
managers tend to ask people for feedback regularly by asking,

"How are we doing?" and later, in presentations, summarize what they have learned with their "stakeholders."

Women's public speaking style can be relational, too. Probably because of the gender socialization process, women prefer talking **with** people, rather than talking at another person or a group. Women appreciate the give-and-take of everyday conversation. As a matter of course, we like to know, "*So, what do you think?*" We do a reality check when we ask, "*How was your experience different from mine?*"

Maybe it's true that women tend to worry more than men do about what others think but, as a result, women speakers are more likely to be concerned about their audience and the impact of their words and ideas on other people. Women speakers do wonder: *How will people react to my ideas?* It is a legitimate concern, and if there is fallout, at least they know they were prepared by predicting the possible consequences.

For many women, communication is a process, not a product. One county government official confided,

> *If I've opened the door and stimulated the listeners to think differently, that's enough for me. It may be a message I need to repeat and repeat in order for people to buy into it. It may be complicated, it may threaten the status quo, and it may cost taxpayers money. It's hubris to think people will change their attitudes in hearing just one presentation. I'm willing to take the time and have the patience necessary to build a solid relationship with my constituents . . . one presentation at a time.*

As a result, she sees public speaking as a way to foster relationships which is often more important than a product. Of course, sometimes, you have no choice. You do need to call for a vote or leave with a check and may not have the luxury of waiting weeks or months for the listeners to take action. When you plan your next presentation, ask yourself:

is my goal to make an immediate impact, or to cultivate a relationship over time?

Good speakers—and this is true of both men and women—aren't aloof. They make the listeners feel "she's one of us." At the podium, both Hillary Clinton and Elizabeth Dole share personal anecdotes and tell stories that illuminate how policy and legislative decisions will play out everyday, for me in my life, for you in your life. Before the presentation, they will be briefed on the demographics of their audience and what people are interested in and worried about. People in sales know that the customer is always thinking, "What's in this for me?" Similarly, when the speaker provides strategic assistance to the listeners—whether it's reassurance, validation, or a list of suggested resources—they are more likely to pay attention and remember what they heard. *When you prepared presentations in the past, did you ever consider the fears, hopes, and dreams of your listeners?*

Good speakers adopt a conversational tone, which is certainly more comfortable for women than a formal one. President Reagan used that approach and was lauded for his success in making each person in his television audience feel as if he were talking directly to her or him. Interestingly, we learned later that speechwriter Peggy Noonan wrote several of Reagan's most quoted speeches.[34]

Women Tend to Express Their Feelings More Than Men Do

In the old days, a familiar image of femininity was of a Victorian woman fainting dead away. Women were said to blush even when they wanted to appear in control; they were highly excitable and cried at the drop of a hat. The stereotypes abound. At the podium, woman speakers today are in control of their feelings but don't flinch from expressing them, particularly when they care about their subject. Personalizing a problem can be an asset when developing a compelling argument for enlisting a group to take action.

Susan Lowell Butler is now an outstanding spokesperson and advocate for ovarian cancer research, perhaps because she was given a poor prognosis when she was initially diagnosed with the disease, and this experience led her to become more proactive. She is now involved in a public relations campaign in which ovarian cancer survivors will unveil an Ovarian Cancer Quilt while physicians and legislators will discuss the latest research opportunities and plan for the future in public forums. Listeners can put a human face on the problem after listening to Susan.

Sharing a personal story that is strategically chosen because it supports your main point can strengthen the presentation. When Geraldine Jensen's former husband moved out of state, she learned that he was no longer legally accountable for child support, and she was forced to become a welfare recipient. As a result of her personal experience, she began an organization called ACES, the Association for Children for Enforcement of Support, for which she has won awards and has received multi-media press coverage. Speaking at conferences and meetings about how non-enforcement affects individual children and families as well as the states, she uses anecdotes from her daily life as a single mother. As a result, audiences believe her. She knows what she's talking about. She speaks about social welfare programs with a guarded sense of humor, discussing what it's like to be on welfare in a down-to-earth way that you and I could relate to.[35] A list of statistics, pie charts, or statistical tables could never make the same lasting impression on her listeners. Don't underestimate how effective it can be to sincerely incorporate feelings of joy, fear, or anger into your presentation. Of course, you will share only what is relevant and the emotions that you can control in order to make your point felt as well as understood.

Kitchen Table Economics Has Value at the Podium

A *Los Angeles Times* article[36] discussing women's future as political leaders stated that there was consensus that women who didn't flinch from those "feminine" sensibilities will succeed in a time of cynicism about government. They identified women's *compassion, sincerity, high ethical standards, good judgment, and a concern for the family.* Journalists believe that the public is concerned with the decline in morals, the safety of children, and basic "kitchen table" economics.

Most people are intimidated by financial reports and budgets. We don't trust our leaders to report information accurately, and that includes money matters. In this climate of cynicism, women's commonsensical and less technical approach to money matters may be particularly appealing in gaining credibility as a presenter. Demystifying complex financial reports in ways that lay people can understand is a skill listeners will appreciate. If you need to speak to your group about money when it isn't your strong suit, gain the technical resources you need and then get answers to the basic questions that lay persons will ask during the Q and A.

Everyone who has tried to balance a household budget knows how to pinch pennies. Women are accustomed to justifying the consequences of financial choices. You know that you can't do everything, so which is it? Can you live with the tough choices made today? For example, you realize the moral implications of taking that decadent trip to Hawaii as opposed to going home for the holidays. Should you take out a loan for the car of your dreams or pay cash for the kids' braces?

Rather than being intimidated by fiscal affairs, women have the potential to be more lively presenters than men when speaking about money. We want to know: what really lies between the spreadsheets? If you meet with people before your next presentation to scope out their financial questions and concerns, you will have time to gather anecdotal material as well as demystify the numbers and stats. Give the financial reports a human face, and your listeners will pay attention.

It's not surprising that Enron's primary whistle blower was a woman, Shereen Watkins, who confronted the CEO on repeated occasions about suspicious corporate accounting practices. Her inability to make an impact on his behavior had a devastating impact on the staff, investors, and the country.[37] These days, and because of her experiences as an Enron insider and a woman executive working within a male culture, she has become a sought-after conference presenter, speaking about the corporate scandal to the media and to Congress.

It's time to realize that women speakers can flaunt what has historically been devalued as the "feminine approach to communication." For our purposes, these traits include but aren't limited to:

- ◆ Valuing relationships and the desire for regular communication
- ◆ Relying on "womanly intuition" and cultivating a sixth sense
- ◆ Expressing feelings
- ◆ Soliciting feedback

◆ Working collaboratively with others and sharing power.

◆ Valuing family life and the skills needed to manage a family

Do any of these traits describe you? You may be surprised to find a broad base of support from strange bedfellows, including both men and women from diverse cultural and racial backgrounds who share your concerns and appreciate your style. Don't underestimate the power of a woman once she is at the podium, being seen and heard as a leader.

LESSON
*Feminine traits can enhance the
speaker's effectiveness.*

Section Three

SPEAKING WITH PASSIONATE CONVICTION

CHAPTER 5

Authenticity

I think that what makes me effective as a person is the same stuff that makes me effective as a speaker, and I think I learned it teaching. That is: If you are to speak with power and integrity, then you cannot be someone else. You cannot act. You must be who you are.[38]
—Susan Lowell Butler,
Women's Health Activist and Advocate

Most women don't have access to the networks and financial resources traditionally reserved for men. As speakers, they have had to rely on the personal resources that they bring to the podium. Authenticity is one of those resources. Women who speak for a living agree: being authentic—communicating your unique self—is the basis for becoming an effective public speaker.

Be Sincere

Think about the last speaker you heard. What made her memorable? More than her words or style, it was probably her sincerity. Regardless of how well she prepared and practiced, she wouldn't have made a lasting impression if she had "attitude." On the other hand, if you want to turn off your audience, be pretentious and affected with an air of superiority.

People know immediately when the speaker is trying to be someone they're not. You might be tempted to blend in with the mainstream by ignoring your cultural background; however, would the average Texan be believed if she spoke with a feigned British accent or vice versa?

Lois recalls that when she graduated from Queens College in New York, she had to pass a diction test to demonstrate that she had mastered Midwestern Speech, which meant sounding like someone from Minnesota.

> *In learning to speak more slowly and lose those infamous New York dentalized "t's" and "d's"—which is a good thing—I became painfully self-conscious. For a time, my speech was stiff and mannered. I had lost my lively style in trying to be someone else.*

Susan Lowell Butler believes you have no choice but to be yourself:

> *You really must. Be the person you are, right there. The power of "being there" doesn't have to be shouted; it is the very essence of power. The audience may not like it. They may reject your ideas. But they will hear you.*

If you prepare yourself to speak to a group by being present, by being in the moment, you will find that you may minimize your anxiety in the process. By being in the present, you're not going to be diffusing your attention worrying about the future. You'll be more ready to handle any question that is thrown at you. For example, when a tough question comes your way, rather than bluffing, you'll realize that it's best to say, "*I really don't know the answer to that one, but I do know this . . . .*" If a mean-spirited confrontation comes at you during the Q and A, you will have the confidence to remain centered while you sort out the situation. You might be able to mobilize your thoughts to tell it like it is:

> *I feel that your question isn't really a question to me but a statement about what **you** believe. You're entitled to*

your opinion, of course. Tonight, however, I'm propos-
ing a new way of thinking about our problem.

Cultivate Self-Awareness

Self-awareness is your ability to be aware of yourself within a particular context. If you are aware of yourself—your strengths, limitations, feelings, anxieties, hot buttons, and physical being—you know you are not exactly like anyone else in your audience. You have a unique spirit and a physical presence. During the presentation, you are in the foreground of the experience, up front and center, and you have a point to make. The audience is in the background of that experience. However, you want to relate, to find that magical place of connection without losing your focus. As a woman, it's easy to focus on what the other person wants to hear. This is your moment to focus on what **you** want to say.

When you are aware of yourself, you know you have certain vulnerabilities and can feel defensive when someone pushes your hot button. Mine may involve being criticized for my competence and credentials, and may lead me to worry about whether I prepared enough. Yours may involve your image and being self-consciousness about your appearance. Being aware of those hot buttons allows a speaker to stay connected to her main points and avoid being derailed by a critical question. Rather than having a panic attack, you might actually come to experience an adrenaline rush when you face a tough question, recognizing the moment as simply another challenge and—no kidding—even enjoyable.

Eleanor Roosevelt was quoted as saying "Remember, no one can make you feel inferior without your consent."[39] It's easy to personalize critical questions or critical feedback. Hearing another person disagree with your position is more about them, and where **they** are coming from than about you. If I can maintain my focus on myself, I find I can navigate through that awkward moment with poise and grace. After taking a deep breath, I might say something like, "That's a different perspective than mine. Here's how I see it," and then move on.

Which of these personal development strategies—and some might seem obvious—would work for you? Check all that apply and note a date to begin one action that will improve your effectiveness as a speaker.

☐ If I wanted to become aware of my level of anxiety about presentations and speeches, I could practice meditation, join a group such as Toastmasters, or practice with small presentations to groups in a safe environment.

☐ If I want to know how other people perceive my speaking style, I can videotape my presentations and review them with a friend or coworker or my supervisor at work.

☐ If I want to be better prepared for how I can relate to my audience, I could consult with someone familiar with that audience, and/or my manager, a mentor, or a coach.

☐ If I want to know what I sound like, I could listen to audiotapes, or improve the range and quality of my voice by studying with a voice teacher.

☐ If I want to become aware of the stories in my life that have been important turning points or have been instructive, I could keep a daily journal that includes photographs.

☐ If I want to know who I am on a deeper level, then I can take personal development courses, read self-improvement books, ask friends for feedback, begin personal counseling, or join a therapy group.

These are a few strategies that will prepare you to know yourself, warts and all. Self-awareness helps you prepare for the day when you master your anxieties about public speaking to face a group or audience because you believe that you have something important to say. When you know who you are, you'll be better able to bounce back from criticism, if there is any, because you can more easily distinguish between the constructive as opposed to irrelevant or mean-spirited criticism. At some point, you will sincerely appreciate the feedback from others that helps you continue to improve your effectiveness as a speaker.

Play to Your Own Strengths

An old Talmudic saying goes:

In some ways, we are like all others; in some ways, we are like some others; in some ways we are like no other.

The adage applies well to the act of delivering a presentation or a speech. You might approach your audience as a woman who has something in common with some of the audience but also, in some ways, has a totally unique set of experiences that defy stereotypical expectations.

As you reflect upon your life experiences—the events that made you the person you are today—consider how you came to care about certain issues. Ask yourself why they matter to you. Be specific. Can you relate to any of these scenarios? If not, write your own.

☐ *Are you interested in advocating for after-school childcare programs because, when your children were very young, you discovered that good, reliable childcare was expensive and difficult—if not impossible—for you and other teachers to find or pay for?*

☐ *Do you want to address the local planning commission on the issue of housing because you and 100,000 others can't find an affordable place to live and must commute two hours a day?*

☐ *Are you asking the PTA to support music in the schools because your at-risk teenager turned her or his life around when he started to play in the band?*

☐ *Do you want to convince your boss to pay for your management training classes because there are no women managers in the agency and you want to advance your career?*

☐ *Do you have a new product line in mind that would turn the company around and save the company from the prospect of a bankruptcy—and you from losing your job?*

☐ *My scenario (insert yours here): _____ .*

Clarifying why you care about an issue or why you want to solve a problem will make it easier for you to be authentic—to be who you are—as you express your feelings and ideas. Your stories will be grounded in concrete experience that no one can argue with. In turn, your sincerity allows the audience to trust you. When you're trusted, you're believed. And the trust you build by relating to the audience will make them more open to changing their point of view and behavior.

Janice Weinman, former executive director of the American Association of University Women, believes that *"Your position [on an issue] comes out of your own experience and the reality from which you come."* Her background as an immigrant, her family's respect for democracy, and their appreciation of economic opportunity have shaped her values and her perception of what's important in the world. No one else could tell her family's story—her experience is unique and indisputable—but the immigrant experience crosses cultural and racial lines.

As a Texas journalist, author and speaker, Liz Carpenter has an outgoing personality. She knows that she is a political animal who has learned how to play to political audiences and loves every minute of it. To her, "politics is an outreach business, and political audiences are gregarious," just as she is. That doesn't mean that you need to be a shoe-pounding politician to get the audience's attention. Carpenter, who was press secretary to former First Lady Lady Bird Johnson, explains that she demonstrated a soft-spoken gentility that came through in every appearance she made as she traveled the country to talk about her beautification project.

> *Lady Bird Johnson didn't like to use humor because she didn't think she could put it over. But she would use a story to break down the walls between people in politics. When she was visiting someone else, she always made him or her feel that it was very special to be there as a guest, and she was always quick to acknowledge a group or person's hospitality, because of her Southern values.*

Witty, gregarious, or gracious, there's no reason not to play up your particular style. *How would you describe yourself? Are you funny or serious? Are you a storyteller or are you better with facts and figures?* Whatever your strengths may be, there's no need for feminine modesty. Instead, once you know who you are, you can cultivate your strengths and use them to make yourself a more effective speaker.

Think of the people you've heard speak who influenced you the most. *Didn't they convince you that they believed in what they were saying—that they were genuinely excited about their topic and concerned about their issue?* They may not have been slick or polished speakers, but if they were prepared, spoke sincerely from the heart and from their own experience, there had to be a moment when you began to care about their issue.

Keep It Real

Paid spokespersons know that if you want to build bridges between groups of people, you should use everyday language, be down to earth, and adopt a conversational tone. Words can build barriers between people. The jargon and acronyms of a particular trade, industry or specialty, or a technical vocabulary can be confusing to listeners who don't share the same work experiences or the same cultural context.

Still an active speaker in her late seventies, Liz Carpenter describes the early meetings of the National Women's Political Caucus:

The women who were the most effective were often Black women who were not used to using trite words like 'structure.' There's not a duller word than 'structure.' They got up and would talk with emotion and passion. They used storytelling and had laughter, too. Their entrance into political speaking was unsophisticated but charming.

California's former Superintendent of Public Instruction Delaine Eastin is a lively and dynamic speaker. She advises people to stick to familiar language and tries to avoid acronyms or prepared sound bytes for the press.

Any materials or language that is unique to a specialization or is technical language can come between you and the audience. You need to realize that you must come across as a person in order to be real and remembered. We can't speak in code.

When you approach a group or an audience, at the heart

of your message is who you are and your point of view as a woman. No matter how much you may appear to be just like the members of a particular audience, there will be something unique about your perspective on the subject. Is there a controversial topic that is of interest to the audience? If so, what's your perspective? Share the information you've gained from reflecting on the roles you play. Ask yourself:

◆ *What do I really think about the new product (or new service)?*

◆ *What did I learn from customers, students, patients, or the children?*

◆ *Do I regret a decision that "we" made this year?*

Audiences find it interesting to hear speakers share how they cope with their own challenges in life, including love, politics, and business.

Women are more forthcoming than men are in terms of sharing information, according to a recent doctoral study at UCLA on gender differences in management styles.[40] Women tend to share what they know in order to empower others. Men, on the other hand, tend to believe that if you give power away, you have less power and status yourself. This attitude is reflected in presentation styles as well, including the way women conduct briefings with their staff. When women managers explain problems in production or customer service, their explanations reflect the value they place on life experiences—their own experiences, and their staff members' and customers' experiences—and they solicit feedback and input from staff. Men tend to present the information and that's all. Take some time now to think about your own experiences and how they might connect you to your audience. *What experiences do you have in common with most others? What experiences in your life make you unique?*

Walking a Fine Line

When a woman cares a great deal about her message, she may be seen as "abrasive" or "having an edge." For example, while progressive women apparently love Senator Barbara Boxer, some of the women we interviewed for this book commented on how Boxer is perceived differently by different audiences. Everyone agreed that her speechmaking skills reflect her intelligence, accomplishments, leadership, and capacity to think on her feet with wit and humor. But she also doesn't compromise when it comes to presenting herself as a hard-core feminist on issues such as reproductive choice. Some whom we interviewed perceive that that image has made it harder for her to gain consensus, even within her own party. On the other hand, Senator Dianne Feinstein supports feminist issues but is not perceived to be an identified feminist. She has figured out a style that works to maintain a tough stand on gun control and has been effective without being described as overly emotional. Women must walk a fine line. Each of us has to be sensitive to the style issues in terms of how to achieve our goals in speaking to a particular audience.

Several years ago, the *Los Angeles Times* did a piece on Los Angeles County Supervisor Gloria Molina, extolling her charisma as a leader but also describing her as having an edge and not being seen as "nice."[41] Clearly, being "nice" would never be an issue for a man. Is this an example of the double standard at work? As Susan Lowell Butler commented:

> *In terms of women speakers being described as "strident" or "shrill," I notice a pattern. Whenever we get very good at what we do, somebody says, "Women are too loud," we're too this, or we're too that. I have never cared a flicker about that. I take it as a compliment.*

CEO Kathleen Drennan is an advocate for increased

research on women's health issues. She is aware of her communication style and knows that although hers is a positive energy, "it can blow people away in the office." Her passion for her work can be misinterpreted as aggressiveness. Conveying to the audience the right sense of emotionality remains a challenge, something to think about as you plan your presentation or speech.

Might listeners interpret your presentation as "strident," "abrasive" or "edgy?" On the other hand, would a man with the same style be effective? Might audiences trivialize your passionate conviction for your issue as that of an overly emotional person? Would you feel compromised if you felt that you had to tone it down for a particular audience?

There's nothing wrong with placing a different emphasis on your topic to meet the needs of the audience. For example, it might make perfect sense to speak to men and women differently about career advancement, housing, saving for retirement, or reproductive choice; however, if you water down your content in a way that misrepresents your beliefs, or modify your assertive style in order to avoid being perceived as strident, you may feel compromised. And the authors would never ask you to compromise your position on an issue in order to be seen as "nice."

Revealing Yourself

A speaker can build trust through self-disclosure, particularly when the anecdote convinces listeners that she's real and that they have something in common. When Betsy Myers ran the Office for Women at the national Small Business Administration (SBA), she found women skeptical about what a Washingtonian could do for them. In order for her to be effective, she had to gain their trust and confidence by convincing them that she could relate to their business predicaments and stresses. She decided to take some risks at the podium and share her personal failures, soon realizing that audiences could identify with her. She began her presentations by telling them the following story about herself.

As a small business owner, Myers didn't realize that the SBA could help her get a bank loan. As a result, at one point she ran up a $22,000 credit card debt. She would tell her listeners: "I woke up one morning and said, 'Why can't I breathe?' In my dreams, I was being suffocated with money." She explains:

> *I knew what it felt like to be lonely in your business and feeling afraid or wanting to quit. Women would line up to talk privately with me afterwards, telling me that they also had ten-, twenty-, forty-thousand-dollar debts. They knew I had been there.*

Myers' authenticity paid off in that she cultivated credibility and built trust. Her audience was then more receptive to everything else she had to say about the SBA.

Comedian, talk show host, and creative consultant to *Rosie* magazine, Rosie O'Donnell took a great risk in speaking to the press about her business problems. In doing so, she gained credibility as a person who struggles with her own moral dilemmas but is capable of taking decisive action. We saw her press conference, sans makeup, giving her side of the story and more of us believed her than if we had merely read it in the papers. Rosie's down-to-earth conversational style and self-effacing humor make her an accessible speaker. In an interview on NBC, O'Donnell said:

> *When I picked this deal I said to them, I am gay and coming out with an ACLU lawsuit in support of the adoption of children in Florida by gay people because I'm a gay foster parent. This company knew exactly*

what they were getting from day one, and what they got was me.[42]

When you stick to your own experience simply told, your listeners can't dispute the personal side of the story.

A caveat is necessary here. Women must watch the temptation to reveal more personal information than is necessary in what appears, at first, to be a relevant anecdote. Women's use of self-deprecating humor is common and can be effective in making you look more human, but it must be used to build you up, not tear you down. A speaker must evaluate the consequences:

◆ *Is telling this anecdote going to help my credibility or weaken it?*

◆ *Will the audience be better able to relate to me and my position or predicament, or will they be turned off?*

Geraldine Jensen, director of ACES, knows how to use humor to transition to the serious subject of collecting child support payments. She always enjoyed being the center of attention: she admits that she was the class clown and a bit of a comedian. She tells audiences the stories about having to finance her new image once her activism reached a national stage and media attention. As a woman who was once on welfare, she rationalized the costs of funding her makeover:

I knew I was in trouble when my glasses, which cost six hundred dollars, cost more than my car. But I need glare-less glasses so that my eyes don't look like coke bottles and distract people from what I'm saying.

Her rise to leadership of the enforcement of child support is more impressive because of her humble beginnings.

Ida Castro cautions that it's important for women to be self-conscious about their passion and to channel that passion in the right direction. There is a fine line between being passionate about your topic and being seen as a passionate person. If a woman becomes too passionate in her speech, the audience might dismiss her as overly emotional, not as analytical about the subject (as a man supposedly would be), and not fully thinking the problem through. While men and women both demonstrate that they can be passionate about a subject they care about, women speakers can lose credibility when they do. Castro believes excessive passion can turn off the audience:

> *More often than not, I can speak from the heart as well as from the mind. When I speak to [an audience that] may not be as friendly, yes, I exercise caution. How do I convey passion without myself being seen as passionate—because when women are seen as just passionate, [the audience doesn't] hear the message. That is the difficulty.*

Women need to stay on message or they will be judged more harshly than a man would for being disorganized. Taking a digression from your prepared remarks is tempting in the apparent comfort of an all-female audience when you assume that you are in a safe harbor and that all the members of the audience are "like you." You may feel comfortable enough that you become conspiratorial, reveal a traumatic incident, or demonstrate self-deprecating humor. Beware! A little bit of self-disclosure can be more than enough and too much self-disclosure can backfire. There are several reasons why.

First, you might digress to the degree that you lose your point with unnecessary details or sidebar comments that take longer than you imagined. Second, sharing upsetting incidents from your past can re-stimulate old feelings and you may lose your composure. This may not be a problem in itself but losing your composure may play into stereotypes about women's tendency to become overly emotional under stress, and this is not the image of a leader that we seek to convey. The audience's perceptions of you "losing your cool" can diminish your credibility and undermine your effectiveness.

The confessional mode is popular in the media and in books for a reason: most of us enjoy being voyeurs. Audiences can naively validate that kind of behavior, which only encourages the speaker to repeat it again. Marie Wilson, Director of the Ms. Foundation, has heard people on the national circuit continually use the podium as personal therapy and take advantage of the audience's good will. Wilson comments on this phenomenon:

There is a line there where talking about your life is really appropriate and the right thing to do. But I've seen some women in enormously high places speak in public in ways I think we shouldn't necessarily be encouraging each other to do, and when taken into another world actually can work against [the speaker].

Alexis Herman is only strategically disclosing. Betsy Myers believes that adds to Ms. Herman's dignity.

She's classy and sophisticated and even a little aloof in that nobody knows a lot about her personal life.

Have you thought strategically about the impact of self-disclosure on your credibility as the voice of authority? Take some time now to decide how much you want to reveal about yourself by checking the boxes that you agree with:

- ☐ *Yes, I'm willing to take the risk of telling my story— it's that important.*
- ☐ *Yes, my personal story is essential to conveying my message.*
- ☐ *Yes, my personal story enhances my credibility as an expert and as a leader.*

☐ *Yes, the climate is safe for me to reveal myself and who I am to the audience.*

☐ *Yes, telling my personal story to my audience isn't self-serving but exemplifies my passionate conviction about my issue.*

Analyzing these factors beforehand is part of a strategy that will allow you to be who you are, an authentic speaker in control of her message.

Know It All (or Most of It, Anyway)

What subject are you most knowledgeable about? The speakers we interviewed indicated that they became public speakers in order to share what they know with others, often beginning with small groups or by observing a mentor speak about a similar subject. When Kathleen Drennan, who is now chair for the Advancement of Women's Health, realized that she knew more about conducting clinical trials than anyone else did, she decided that she was an authority on the subject and was ready to speak up. At that point, people began taking her seriously. As President and CEO of The Chicago Center for Clinical Research, Drennan says that once she learns something new, she shares it with as many people as she can. As a result of this tendency, she has gotten into the habit of speaking regularly about current developments in the industry with her staff, colleagues, and other clinical directors. She is now a sought-after public speaker.

She advises others who have developed expertise on a particular subject to "dare to be bold." She admits:

I have never given a talk without including some edge of controversy. This has left some people not agreeing with me, and some people thinking the presentation was fabulous!

Boldness has its price. Each audience scopes you out from head to toe. Who you are and what you stand for will be part of their assessment of your credibility. Do you know what you're talking about? Do you care about what you're talking about? Why should they care?

Marie Wilson, believes that the audience will peg you based on "whom you choose to affiliate your life with and stand up for at the podium."

> *The real power of a presentation is how much of your whole self is sitting there—appropriately balanced, because it is an energy field. Those of us who speak well can stand up and speak well almost under any circumstances, but you know when you're really present . . . and there's an enormous difference.*

Take some time now to think about the issue that inspires your passion. *What do you personally know to be true because you're an insider? What new insights do you have? What stories and anecdotes can you share? What would surprise or inspire the audience? How can you convince the audience that their ignorance about this issue may be costly? How can you further enhance your knowledge to become even more of an expert on this issue?*

Whose Words Are They?

Imagine the opportunity to hand over an assignment to someone else, as presidents do, and tell him or her to write you a great speech. Peggy Noonan discussed her experiences when she was writing for Ronald Reagan in *What I Saw At the Revolution*. Reagan's rhetorical voice was as much Peggy Noonan's as it was his—maybe more so (at times) considering how gifted a writer she is.[43] The fact that a speechwriter's position is a full-time job indicates that the role is valuable.

As a result, we were amazed when the women speakers we interviewed said they prefer not to delegate the task but to write their speeches themselves. This ensured that they would be comfortable with the speech and could deliver their stories and key points authentically, from the heart.

Many professional speakers and leaders told us that they don't read written speeches or prepared texts but rather speak from outlines, note cards, or completely from memory.

There are plenty of good speechwriters out there; even if you use one, however, the best speakers know their subject backward, forward, and upside down. Perhaps more importantly, they know themselves in relation to the subject. And they know the point they want to get across. They know what kind of speech will grab the audience by the shoulders and shake them out of complacency or lethargy, gently or passionately, until the speaker's point of view is seen and heard.

People in public positions certainly can live to regret it if they impulsively go off on a tangent. Yet each of the women we interviewed wanted to speak in her own voice without using a prepared manuscript. Betsy Myers admitted that, even at the White House, she rarely if ever used the speechwriter in her own office because she did her best work when she wrote her speeches herself.

Kathleen Drennan's passion about and knowledge of women's health motivates her to speak up. Sharing is second nature to her. "If I have a new hairdresser, I share the information with ten people. If I have something new, I share it with ten people."

She writes out very little beforehand because she knows her subject so thoroughly. In fact, she believes that she does better when she shoots from the hip, "meaning that they are not canned presentations." She adds that in formal presentations, " I don't do as well because I can lose the passion and authenticity."

Susan Lowell Butler is also very confident about what she knows, and admitted that she frustrated her staff:

Speechwriters would track me down and kill me. I had speechwriters on my staff many times and I finally said, 'Just give me the research. I'll put the ideas together myself.'

Ann Stone, media trainer and president of Republicans for Choice, prefers to dictate her speeches in order to capture the flavor of her conversational voice, relying on someone else to type the material. Liz Carpenter relies on an outline but tries to speak off-the-cuff, using time-tested stories and Texas regional humor as often as possible. Each of these speakers wants her public voice to reflect authenticity.

Speak in your own words. You have your idiomatic expressions, regional dialects, and slang. Talk to golfers about a frog's hair or flying eyebrows. We know what we mean when told to 'hold your horses,' that 'he's a bump on a log' or 'she's a bat out of hell.'[44] We may not know the origins of old expressions, but they'll be familiar to a particular audience. Your mama's stories, your regionalisms, accents, favorite films and novels, melody, cadence, and rhythm—these expressions and sounds are part of who you are. A speechwriter, as good as he or she may be, cannot get inside your head, cannot mimic your mannerisms or flaunt the nuances in your speech patterns. No one can "make you" authentic, and that's what we're talking about here: authenticity. Know your subject, your audience, and yourself, and then speak with passionate conviction. Talk about what you truly believe in. Trust yourself. That's what really matters.

Come As You Are, but Also Dress the Part

Whether you deliver a presentation to your staff, a group, or association, the first impression begins with your appearance, so do give it some thought. "Dress for success" books abound, so we won't dwell on the details of having your colors done or suggest that you wear a red power-suit. Suffice it to say that you want to walk a fine line between (1) standing out in a positive way and (2) looking like members of the audience. You don't want anything to come between you and your ability to cultivate a relationship with your audience.

Sometimes the best strategy is to identify with the audience. Now in her mid-thirties, Laura Groppe, founder and CEO of Girl Games, Inc., faces particular challenges in establishing credibility. Her audiences run the gamut from pre-teen consumers and their parents to sophisticated and skeptical venture capitalists. While remaining true to herself—staying authentic—she varies her look to fit her audience by dressing like them.

> *Because I'm relatively young, when I face an audience of girls, I match them in appearance. I'll wear blue lipstick, high tops, and a tiara. When I face a more mature audience (for example, of venture capitalists), I look more corporate. I do think about these things beforehand.*

Others indicated that they dress down or dress up depending on the audience and the occasion. Speakers consider how they'll look if the event will be televised or videotaped, because television and news media seem to add ten pounds to the speaker. In any case, there is a great deal of leeway for individual choice.

In the past, when fewer women were working outside the pink-collar ghettos, it was common for women who wanted to be seen and heard to dress like and sound like men. Today, it is possible to dress like a woman, manage like a woman, and sound like a woman.

Take some time now to think about your appearance.
Take our little quiz:

1. *Do you dress appropriately for your age, audience, and
    your subject?* ___ *Yes* ___ *No* ___ *Not Sure*
2. *Are you dressing like a male clone?*
    ___ *Yes* ___ *No* ___ *Not Sure*
3. *Does your appearance project the real you?*
    ___ *Yes* ___ *No* ___ *Not Sure*
4. *Is there an outfit that reflects your cultural heritage?*
    ___ *Yes* ___ *No* ___ *Not Sure*
5. *Does your style of dress and appearance support your
    verbal message?* ___ *Yes* ___ *No* ___ *Not Sure*

Bragging is difficult for those of us socialized to be modest, and it is no small leap to take your success stories public.
It may be awkward to brag in public about your accomplishments and explain why your perspective on an issue is intelligent, visionary, and worthy of an audience's attention.
Bragging is certainly not part of women's early socialization
as a "feminine" human being. Janice Weinman admits:

> *I am least good at talking about myself. When you run
> for public office, that [lack of skill] is a great liability. I
> would much prefer to talk about issues and what other
> people think and do rather than about myself. But I
> think that communicating about yourself is a very
> important connector with an audience .... The kind of
> personal position you take is relevant to your political
> position on an issue. Your position comes out of your
> experience and the reality from which you come.*

Given her professional demeanor, many accomplishments, and impressive educational background, it is hard to
imagine how Weinman might not be an intimidating presence. Yet her role of executive director required her to con-

nect with diverse AAUW members across the country. She focuses on what she has in common with her multicultural audiences. Like many women in her audience, she:

◆ has lived all over the country

◆ has attended public schools throughout her life

◆ is the child of immigrants and understands how difficult it is to adjust to a new culture

◆ believes deeply in educational opportunities for girls and women.

Dr. Weinman considers her best speech to be her AAUW inaugural address in which she shared her cultural background and organizational vision, and emphasized her own convictions.

Will authentic women speakers find that male audiences are also receptive to their stories and can relate to their concerns? We can't ignore the facts that, as women's roles are changing, men's roles in society are changing, too, although perhaps not fast enough for some. As increasing numbers of men work alongside women, become divorced, marry career women, and have to live with the challenges from educated and/or liberated daughters, it will be easier for women speakers to find issues of common concern to connect with male audiences.

In fact, we must entertain the possibility that women and men may have more—not less—in common in the twenty-first century, and more to say to one another as well. No matter what the composition of the audience, your authenticity will see you through. Be who you are and they will listen.

LESSON
Know yourself, be yourself.

CHAPTER 6

Early Influences

My aunt won a speech contest many years ago and I grew up listening to people [like her] tell wonderful stories at family gatherings. Stories are a wonderful way to get people to hear and remember our message. It was very important for me to grow up hearing outstanding storytellers and knowing what that sounded like because they became role models for me in my professional career.
— Delaine Eastin, Former California
State Superintendent of
Public Instruction

Many influences shape your readiness to stand up and speak your mind. The lessons learned from the speakers we interviewed suggest that self-confidence builds over time. Early influences that shape a girl's or woman's development can prepare her to manage the fear of public speaking that is common to most people. Given that it is likely that audiences will be more critical of women speakers than men, however, what factors can increase a woman's self-confidence in the role of public speaker?

Family Members

The role of loving and supportive parents and siblings on a girl's self-confidence can't be overstated. People who know that they have a secure place in the world are more willing to take risks to express what's on their minds. After all, if there's rejection by an indifferent or harsh world, parents or siblings can provide consistent reassurance and comfort. Audiences can be receptive, neutral, or rude. Speaking up at the dining table is good preparation for speaking up in the council chambers or in the boardroom. Not every presentation goes perfectly well. Some fall flat. After a disappointing presentation when you couldn't think on your feet, how do you land on your feet emotionally?

Betsy Myers, who achieved a leadership role with the Welfare to Work initiative in the Clinton administration, had a supportive family.

We had a mother who told us that we were wonderful all the time and that we could do anything, which made a huge difference. Our father was more a disciplinarian. He was a navy guy and from him we learned about discipline and hard work.

She feels nostalgic about her childhood experiences and sees all of the sisters as the overachiever types. "Between the three girls we shared love and support and really stood by each other's side."

The Myers daughters had opportunities to work on a national stage early in life without the usual amount of seasoning that allows people to weather the intensity of a 24/7 political lifestyle. Her younger sister, Dee Dee Myers, achieved success in her twenties as Bill Clinton's campaign manager and press secretary, and later as an MSCNBC television commentator and political editor of *Vanity Fair* magazine. Without those old-fashioned values to ground them, they could have quickly failed in their very public lives. Betsy believes that neither she nor her sister had much confidence in their ability to speak in public to start with but they were forced into public speaking as a result of having political success so early in life.

School experiences also provided excellent preparation for being in the public eye later in life. Betsy was more political than her sister.

> As a girl, I was always a real people-person, always active in groups and, in fact, even ran for office in school. Dee Dee is more of an introvert [and] . . . . I am much more extroverted. I go out and get all my energy from people.

Betsy sees that all of the sisters have continued to develop themselves in their thirties. She and Dee Dee "have often talked about the reasons we are able to take some risks in our lives," like moving to Washington, D.C., or selling a business. "I always knew that if worse came to worst, I could go live with either of my sisters and they would take care of me, and the same thing for them." Safety nets—whether family, friends, or financial cushions—allow people to take risks in their public and professional lives, knowing that they won't crash and burn. Speaking up for what you believe in, particularly if it's an unpopular position, is certainly one of those risks.

Ann Stone, founder of Republicans for Choice, was raised by a loving and supportive mother and grandmother. Although she lived at the edge of poverty and wore hand-me-down clothes, she credits her extended family for helping her mother succeed as a single parent, and in particular, her grandmother who made sure that daily routines in the household worked.

While it was very difficult for her mother to be a single parent, Ann reflected that she "never knew that was supposed to be a problem." Her mother convinced her to work hard enough to get straight 'A's in school and then promised that she wouldn't have to do housework. She admits that public speaking "was natural for me, but part of that was due to a mother who convinced me to do something that I felt I couldn't do." This is similar to what Ann tries to do as a speaker: influence audiences to do things that they feel are impossible.

Congresswoman Loretta Sanchez credits her dad for encouraging her to take speech classes. Soon she entered competitions, reciting other people's work and winning awards. Now that she writes her own material, she finds the speaking situation quite different but appreciates what she learned from her early classroom experiences.

Susan Lowell Butler grew up in Long Island, New York, and was given lots of loving support by parents who were professional, successful, and positive role models. Because she was the only child, she had lots of attention.

I didn't know that I was a girl and that I was supposed to fail. I wasn't raised in a conventional way. I was raised as a human . . . . Since I was an only child . . . we did things like go fishing together. I was "the kid." I didn't grow up in an atmosphere of "because you're a girl, you can't . . ." or "Be afraid." So I didn't. Until my '20s, I had no perception that there were probably things other people thought I couldn't or shouldn't do. It was great.

Her parents would ground her if she didn't perform, so she "was tremendously motivated." Butler believes that her public school experiences, combined with her home environment, helped her to develop her intellect and communication skills. Later she went on to become a teacher herself. What she learned from teaching was that you had to be yourself "because kids have an immediate bullshit detector." She is known for her tell-it-like-it-is candid and direct style, both in conversation and at the podium.

CEO of GirlGames, Inc., Laura Groppe's parents were role models for her because speaking was a requirement of their business life and activism.

My mother was very involved in the Houston Women's Center and had a passion for her work as an activist. I know that when you're passionate about something, you exude confidence. If you saw me speak, you'd be able to see how much I care. My present situation is a luxury. I get to make a difference in girls' lives. Of course I can really get behind this product.

Groppe is now an enthusiastic speaker who is passionate about her software product for girls, facing a range of audiences that include girls, parents, venture capitalists, women's groups, and business groups.

Former California Superintendent of Public Instruction Delaine Eastin appreciates how her family tradition of storytelling influenced her speaking style. She's comfortable making her point by sharing a personal anecdote. For instance, when Eastin spoke to a group of supporters in an informal setting, she told a story about her parents' post-World War II generation, and the foresight they had to invest in taxing themselves to build California's educational system, which became the best in the nation. "My father would have mortgaged his home to send me to UC Davis," she confided. "He didn't have much himself, but he knew the value of an education."

Texan Liz Carpenter grew up with people who loved language. Her mother quoted poetry and "had six years of Latin, so we also heard a lot of Tennyson and Kipling. This stayed with me." It's not surprising that Carpenter went on to become a journalist and speechwriter, and her speeches utilize regionalisms and alliterative language.

At an AAUW convention in June 1997, Executive Director Janice Weinman reminisced about the importance

of maternal encouragement at a choice point in her life thirty
years earlier.

> When I announced my plans to attend graduate school,
> a professor told me, "Janice, don't waste your time and
> money." Fortunately, I turned for counsel and courage
> to my mother, a woman who bravely balanced family
> and career. She told me to keep on keeping on, and that
> is why I stand before you here today. When my daugh-
> ter graduated high school, I asked myself: How can I do
> for her what my mother did for me, to offer her the con-
> fidence to believe she can do whatever she sets out to do
> and be whatever she sets out to be?[45]

Theater Experience

Several women interviewed for this book had unique experiences that have helped them develop poise and feel comfortable onstage. Both communications consultant Susan Lowell
Butler and former California Superintendent of Public
Instruction Delaine Eastin were trained in theater during
their childhood and high school years. Those experiences
taught them how to project their voices, emphasize words,
and phrases, deliver punch lines, tell stories, and "read" and
react to an audience. Both women think of public speaking as
a role they play; they know that performance-anxiety is normal, so they take it in stride.

Although Susan Lowell Butler was involved in a lot of
theater productions in college as well as summer theater, she
says that she's not really an actress. Rather, she loves the dramatic nature of life itself.

> I'm just Susan in wigs. I am a director. That's what I
> love. All my life that's what I have done and do. I direct
> and produce things, make stuff happen. I love chaos. I

love to rescue. Call me when you're desperate, when
you're hanging from a ledge.

At the age of twenty-six, Susan was a natural to become
the first field crisis organizer for the National Education
Association (NEA), a job that led her to travel all over the
country, including Hawaii and Alaska. She compensated for
her youth and ignorance by being prepared and working
extremely hard, and says that she had a great time. This was
the kind of job that thrust her into the public eye, allowing
her to learn how to think on her feet, deal with controversy,
and, in short, use everything she had.

By her twenties, she had acquired high standards of performance, the poise and composure she learned from drama
studies, her "can-do" attitude, and, in particular, her lack of
self-consciousness about being a woman in a leadership role.
That's probably why she was named director of communications for NEA, the biggest teachers' union in the U.S., at
twenty-nine. As a person who loved making things happen,
she found that she was a natural spokesperson, managing
dramatic crises and leading people through occasional disas-
ters to positive outcomes.

Activist Geraldine Jensen always liked being the center of
attention and knows that she was a bit of an actress as a child,
admitting:

[I have] always been the class clown and a comedian. I
like to use a tremendous amount of humor. . . . You
learn what people laugh at. You learn you can feel the
audience and how they are responding to you.

In building her organization that seeks to correct
inequities in child support payments, acting skills are helpful.
Jensen has had to stay cool and remain strong when dealing
with contentious audiences who want to tear her down, challenge her authority, and question her motives. Her work is

not for the faint at heart.

Although she has a gregarious and assertive personality today, Delaine Eastin describes herself as an introvert as a young child, "someone who didn't have a presence." Mr. Deck, her high school drama teacher, provided the first bit of encouragement to express herself . He encouraged her to try out for a play called *The Man Who Came to Dinner*. This was a turning point in her life because "it helped me to understand how to play a role, and develop presence and poise on stage."

Debate Skills

Confidence gained from theater classes and stage productions led Delaine Eastin to participate in the school's Debate Club the following year. Drama, debate, and storytelling skills served her well as she campaigned and had to challenge conventional thinking as well as public complacency and cynicism about public education. She was able to communicate with diverse audiences, even in politically charged debates. Later, once elected, she delivered eloquent formal speeches to the legislature, at conferences, or commencement addresses.

By the time she was a sophomore in high school, Ann Stone knew she enjoyed participating in debates. She considers this training extremely important, especially later in the rough-and-tumble world of political activism. Ann Stone's mother, who completed her GED after dropping out of school, was a tremendous role model because she never was afraid and told Ann to never be afraid. Perhaps this is why Ann has been described as a fearless debater, even in controversial televised debates. As the founding director of Republicans for Choice, pro-choice activists who are members of both parties have praised her:

I am one of the few who can think on my feet and not

be intimidated by anything . . . . I get sent out to be the
spokesperson because of my debate training.

Dorothy Ann Willis was such a skilled debater in high school that she won a debate scholarship to Baylor University. She later went on to become governor of Texas, and we know her as Ann Richards. Never one to pull punches, she criticized her opponent for the governorship in her bid for re-election by saying "George [Bush] can't help himself. He was born with a silver foot in his mouth."

Ida Castro, the former executive director of the Equal Employment Opportunity Commission (EEOC), believes that she developed comfort with public speaking by debating the issues with her father every evening after he finished work. Because her parents worked long hours, she wanted to make every minute count. Her father loved to discuss current events and quizzed them thoroughly. By age six, Ida and her older brother got up early every morning and read two newspapers in order to be ready to discuss such heady topics as statehood for Puerto Rico, civil rights in America, Sputnik, and U.S.-Russian relations. Castro reminisced about these debates:

> *Very early on, I learned to be very opinionated in a*
> *strange sort of way. In terms of standing up for what I*
> *believe in, I was the smallest one and had to have an*
> *articulate position that wasn't ridiculous . . . yet differ-*
> *ent enough for anyone to want to listen to it . . . . My*
> *father and mother always expected us to defend our*
> *position . . . . And if you expressed your opinion and*
> *weren't able to defend it, then that was stupid, and in*
> *my family, being stupid was not a good thing.*[46]

Castro also appreciates the value of education and equal opportunity because her parents "have struggled all their life to get whatever it is that they have in an honorable way."

Castro wants to "help the millions of people, just like mom and pop" who deserve a break. The lively debates at the kitchen table and in front of the television helped Ida Castro prepare to be seen and heard when speaking to Congress.

Work

Work can provide a powerful impetus to bloom as a speaker, particularly when a woman's job or role forces her into the limelight. When Susan Lowell Butler became a union organizer, she quickly realized that she had people's lives at stake.

> *All the people running the union were men. And there was me, big bosom, long black hair, and not a clue. Next thing you know, I'm on the bargaining team, writing the propaganda, and stirring up the troops. I had enough of the skills to grow into the role . . . . I also got to grow up, because when you stand up in front of 800 people and say, 'We're going to go on strike,' you'd better grow up.*

Butler learned that hers was the voice of authority. When she said, "Strike," her audience knew she meant business.

On her first day of work at the Small Business Administration (SBA) office, Betsy Myers' boss, Friskan Ball, warned her that she was going to spend 60 percent of her time out on the road giving speeches, talking, listening, and doing media. Her reaction: "Oh, my god!"

> *So I listened to him because he is a great speaker. I listened to his vision at SBA and fit my speeches to mesh with what he was doing because his vision aligned with what the president was doing. I did a lot of public speaking, and I learned.*

One of the opportunities provided by working in a national program is the opportunity to see and hear other

speakers besides the woman's own colleagues and boss—
both men and women—and learn from them what works
and what doesn't. Learning from watching talented as well as
deadly, dull speakers was part of Myers' education as a
speaker. At a business lunch meeting, Betsy was painfully
aware of the difference:

> One was so boring I could hardly listen to him, and the
> other had me on the edge of my chair. The second one,
> Fred Grandy, who played Gopher on "The Love Boat,"
> is an ex-congressman and now is CEO of Goodwill
> Industries. Honestly, I would have signed up for any-
> thing when he finished speaking. He . . . had a guarded
> sense of humor. Goodwill works with a lot of disabled
> people, and so he was telling stories about the people
> [they work with].

She soon realized that "the audience wonders: what does
this mean to me and how can I relate?" When she was talking
about government programs or initiatives to people out in
the country, outside of Washington, D.C., she realized that
she had to bring complex topics down to their level of understanding. The speaker's job, she believes, is to make the material matter to the listeners. Even dry, technical material can
be presented meaningfully so that it is remembered by a listener; for example, even a percentage of an interest point difference can matter a great deal to someone trying to get out
of credit card debt.

Kathleen Drennon worked her way up the ladder in the
pharmaceutical field without a Ph.D. or M.D., until the day
she began her own business conducting clinical trials.
Experience from working with male bosses taught her how to
be in charge and communicate assertively.

> I had a lot of mentors and they were all men, because
> that's all there were in the field, but they were willing to

help. I never suffered from having male mentors.

Most of us have male bosses so it's important to remember that we can learn new skills and techniques by observing any and every good speaker.

Ida Castro recalls that she also developed confidence as a speaker through trial by fire when she taught labor education courses at Rockhurst College. Facing classes, thinking on her feet, developing the ability to recall information and provide explanations—all this proved invaluable. In addition, she gained confidence by doing labor arbitration and political campaigning for people like Mayor David Dinkins in New York City.

Even if you don't work for a mayor, your work setting provides you with a "laboratory" to practice delivering brief presentations and improve your skills by soliciting feedback from peers and managers. It's better to have your trial by fire when there are no reporters in the room.

Early influences on the speaker can help shape her attitudes about exercising her right to free speech, even if doing so means being unpopular. The lucky ones among us gained communication skills and a positive "can-do" attitude early in life from family members and teachers. Of course, one can always find mentors, take classes, and watch good speakers to make up for lost time. It's easy to develop new communication skills and self-confidence when you have a reason to be seen and heard.

LESSON
*Early influences develop a speaker's
self-confidence.*

CHAPTER 7

Subjective to Strategic Preparation

There are times when you bring people to their feet, when you bring people to tears, and when you bring people to new insights . . . where people have made psychic change, money change, and real change in their lives. I've had women come up and say, "I've heard you and I've never been the same." You want that to be the experience every time. That is also a part of being seen, being heard, and being real, for yourself.
—Marie Wilson, Director of the Ms. Foundation[47]

There are some important differences between conversing and speaking in public. Facing a large audience is filled with many unknowns. The presenter doesn't have the flexibility found in the give-and-take of social conversations or business discussions; that is, if the listener looks horrified when you express your position, you can always find out why or change the subject. It's not so easy when all eyes are on you, the speaker, delivering a monologue.

Asserting yourself as a public speaker is risky for any speaker, particularly for women who value their personal relationships and don't want to be embarrassed later by something they said in public. They may catastrophize that people will take offense at their ideas to the point of losing friends, respect, or their jobs. However, it is true that women are more vulnerable than men to audience criticism because the speaker role is in conflict with the feminine sex role. What we were programmed to do in public was to smile, be nice, defer to men, and avoid stirring up disagreements or fueling a conflict. In addition, our own concerns about walking that fine line—that is, not being seen as too forceful, opinionated, boastful, self-aggrandizing, or perceived as "masculine"—may exacerbate anxiety and self-consciousness. We haven't had the psychological or educational preparation necessary to feel comfortable at the front of the room speaking from a podium. Therefore, preparation is the key to a woman's success as a speaker, beginning with her attitude.

Think about the issues that are near and dear to your heart. What's bugging you? Check those items below that apply or make up your list:

☐ Are you a parent debating the viability of providing an on-site childcare center with your employer?

☐ Do you need to convince your local school district to offer after-school drama arts classes?

☐ Are you a scientist seeking funding for groundbreaking research?

☐ Are you a project team leader trying to gain consensus about using a new technology?

☐ Are you the president of an association or board of directors trying to increase and diversify your membership?

☐ Are you advocating for access to mammograms for poor women?

☐ Do you believe that your company or agency should provide English as a Second Language (ESL) classes on-site in order to improve communication and productivity ?

☐ Do you need to raise money for your favorite candidate—or for your own campaign?

If the shoe fits, step up to the podium. You're on. Eyes and ears are focused on you, waiting to hear what you have to say. You want to succeed, but do you know how to prepare yourself? From avoiding the media minefields to breaking through the double-bind, there are lessons to be learned from successful women leaders—our role models—that will help women to speak more confidently in a public voice.

Erase the Old Tapes

All women interviewed agreed with recent research on women's communication styles, which inform us that women—even competent, very intelligent women—tend to be more tentative than men are. And yet, to paraphrase an old quotation, "the speaker who hesitates is lost." Susan Lowell Butler says that:

> Men assume that you want to hear them. Women are more tentative. And often even a very good female speaker will take kind of a long time to get to the point. The top speakers don't do that. The top speakers have their opening lines in their head. They're prepared. They're ready. They're not at all tentative. To do that in a conversation is bad enough.

Women must believe that their ideas are important enough to share with others. Charlotte Beers, chair and CEO of the advertising agency, Ogilvy & Mather, writes:

> It's important that women believe that we can make a difference. Believing that, and in the power of the individual, is great weaponry to influence the marketplace.[48]

Why is it difficult to be bold and outspoken? First, it's difficult when you've not been encouraged to have big dreams, much less talk about them. Were you prepared to think about your future and set goals for yourself? Think back to your early years. Would you enter "yes" to any of these questions?

☐ *Did the third grade teacher or your parent put a kibosh on your dream of being a scientist, engineer or ____ ?*

☐ *Did the guidance counselor redirect you from a law career to secretarial school?*

☐ *Did religious or cultural traditions define the role of women in your family to be subordinate to men?*

☐ *Did you grow up listening to music that suggested that you needed a man in order to be a "real" woman?*

Until the second wave of feminism, and sex discrimination legislation such as Title VI and Title IX of the Civil Rights Act, women were not educated to think of themselves as having anything important to say or to consider a wider range of formerly all-male occupations or professional roles. Whether they were secretaries, stewardesses, nurses, waitresses, cheerleaders, or moms, women were used to serving, caring for, and standing behind other people—mainly men—who moved into decision-making and leadership roles in business, politics, or the professions—architecture, medicine, law, education, and government. Women typically worked behind the scenes; they typed other people's words, cared for the sick, cooked, cleaned, and served, waved, cheered, and tended children. They didn't run companies or run for office and it was the rare woman who delivered a presentation or a speech.

Second, being bold and outspoken is difficult if you were not encouraged to speak up by parents, teachers, friends, or mentors. Think back to your early years. Check the boxes that are true or add your own descriptions:

☐ *People in my family would solicit my opinion or ask me what I thought.*

☐ *People told me that I was worth listening to.*

☐ *I watched movies or read books about women in unconventional roles.*

If you lacked encouragement in your early years, public speaking can be a scary proposition. Being direct in expressing your opinion is a particularly tough role for a woman who has lacked encouragement or role models. The possibility of being seen as smart and superior goes against everything women learned about being "modest." Being feminine and being smart just didn't add up. By contrast, ask yourself: "Would a man worry about being seen as "too smart?" Not a chance. Case closed.

The messages—explicit or subtle—that females received about being "nice" are hard to erase, but you do have a choice in the matter. You could bite your tongue out of deference to those old messages, but why would you? If you want to be effective speaking to a group from the front of the room, you'll have to reject those old tapes about what you can and can't do as a woman. Being nice, modest, and self-effacing will inhibit you from taking a position, particularly one that is unpopular. However, if you choose to follow your heart and speak your mind, your life will surely unfold in unexpected ways that defy the limitations of convention.

Evaluate what might be lost if you didn't speak up about an important issue at meetings or public events, and then decide if the risks are worth it. Whether local or global, you have important ideas to share. Pick a topic or add your own. Can you make the case for why your organization needs to adopt one of the following proposals by giving three reasons why each proposal is a win-win solution:

◆ *Everyone benefits from a new on-site childcare center.*

◆ *Everyone benefits from a new product (or service) that will make our company (or agency) more successful.*

◆ *Everyone benefits from better security for evening shift workers.*

◆ *Everyone benefits from more flexible work schedules for women and men.*

◆ *Everyone benefits from advocating for more affordable housing for police, teachers, and firefighters.*

◆ *Everyone benefits from* _____ .
(insert idea)

You may not have been encouraged to speak up in the past but you now have years of experience and great ideas to share. Accept the fact that your aversion to the podium may be coming from a lack of encouragement—as well as a double standard for girls and women. While that would be understandable, those old scripts may be holding you back from realizing your dreams. Realize that your good ideas could improve the local economy, public schools, your community, and, ultimately, change the world. All great ideas had to overcome profound skepticism. Yours is a new voice at the table. Your new attitude should be: *I want to be seen and heard.*

Strategically Prepare Your Ideas for a Public Hearing

Men are expected to be logical, whether or not they always are. As a woman, you must be strategic in demonstrating that you're a logical thinker. Your ideas must be easy to follow and hang together. You need to remain focused on the overarching topic with examples, quotes, statistics, and the development of your various key points. Whether they scratch out ideas on a notepad or index cards, effective speakers organize their ideas into an outline. Many speakers highlight their key points in yellow and write "reminders" in the margins in red. Men may have the luxury of rambling, but women don't.

Whether you speak about the complexities of a broad social policy or how to use new software, there's always more to say than time will allow. Given how many variables are involved in speaking to groups and audiences, it's better to be safe than sorry. Have your information at your fingertips in whatever media works best for you: paper, slides, index cards, or PowerPoint software. Number each sheet or slide so that you won't lose your place.

Attorney Angela Oh starts a file for each presentation and collects articles and materials that become incorporated into her outline. She jots down ideas on a yellow pad, includes reference to research studies, and makes a list of her relevant personal experiences. She reviews the folder before the presentation or speech, but she doesn't write out her full speech. Instead, she speaks off-the-cuff and, once at the podium, weaves all of her ideas and experiences together. She'd never write out a speech word-for-word unless it's for the most formal presentation. She thinks of speaking to an audience as a conversation that will continue without end. She hopes that:

> . . . our paths will cross again. I think out loud about what I want to say, rather than having a particular technique, considering what each particular audience wants from me.

Every speaker has to find what organizing strategy works for her. We're all busy these days and most women are juggling many roles.

You and I prepare for a dinner party in our own ways. Similarly, you and I will have different strategies that work for us as we prepare for a presentation. Even if you're anxious about public speaking, don't be tempted to use a typed manuscript to manage anxiety; it will prevent you from having the positive adrenaline rush that comes from excitement. You'll want to make authentic contact with your audience in a conversational, lively manner.

Liz Carpenter feels that speaking from notes gives her greater confidence than trying to deliver a prepared manuscript. She refers to her notes but doesn't read them word-for-word, believing that "this is where businessmen blow it. They read the speech, pre-typed." She underlines key words in red to remind herself what to emphasize so that the audience will remember it.

How do you convey confidence in your expertise? Preparation is the key. You might try to predict the questions in the audience member's mind, questions that you should be prepared to answer. For instance, think about the need for a childcare center at the local industrial complex. You might have strong feelings about the need to find funding for such a center, long overdue in your neighborhood, but you don't want to stop at the feelings level. You want something done about the situation. Use the following categories to discuss the positive and negative aspects of your proposal, space, money, time, and human impact:

1. *Address the pro's and con's. What are the pros and cons of having a childcare center close to work for recruiting and retaining working parents?*

2. *Paint a visual picture. How would you design it, from front to back?*

3. *Deal with the costs. How much will the childcare center cost and how could monies be raised?*

4. *Think about time. How long will it take, from a best-case to worst-case scenario?*

5. *Finally, consider the human aspect of any change. What
   is the impact on our people if we go forward in terms of
   a best-case and worst-case scenario?*

Going through this exercise will prepare you to handle the
dynamics of the Q and A, after your monologue is over.

Just the Facts, Ma'am

Imagine yourself at the front of the room, about to begin
your presentation. You are the epitome of Cool, anything but
the hysterical, "feminine" woman who has been stereotyped
for centuries as lacking the capacity to be logical. Having
facts to back up your opinion is an essential strategy for
increasing the audience's confidence in you as a balanced,
rational leader when things get tough and the tough get going.
It's particularly important for the woman speaker to have current, accurate facts and statistics to back up her position and
point of view. You can have a lot of great anecdotes and legitimate feelings about your subject but without the facts to support your proposal, you'll probably lose your audience.

   You need to be able to discriminate between what is common knowledge and your unique knowledge stemming from
your unique life experience. People will want to hear a new
slant, a new voice. Being confident about what you know
isn't enough. You need to be clear in your own mind about
what needs to be done about the problem or the issue, no
shilly-shallying about it. Then, ask yourself if you have
explained your position precisely.

   ◆ *What change do I want to see happen?*
   ◆ *When do I want to see it happen?*
   ◆ *What are the very specific pros and cons of having this
     change happen?*

◆ *How dramatically can I convey my points, with anecdotes, stories, and statistics?*

Once you're clear about your position on an issue, you'll need to support your point of view with *the most current research* on the problem and then explain your position in concrete terms. This is particularly important in terms of our fast-paced, information-driven, global economy, ever-changing high-tech world. Ask yourself:

◆ *What percentages, statistics, pie charts, and graphs will visualize the pros and cons of my position?*

◆ *What new or controversial research challenges the status quo?*

Whatever you do, be direct about what *you* think, feel, and know to be true. When you second-guess the audience, you can lose your clarity and focus. Stop worrying about what other people will think about you. What do *you* know? Figure this out, and you'll be less tempted to step into the trap of tentativeness that is common to many women.

Think of a reporter sitting in the audience covering your talk. *Will you give her interesting new information for her quotes or, instead, will she capture one of those mushy off-the-record "sort-of, kind-of" remarks?* As you craft your remarks, develop quotable phrases that rhyme or are easy to remember. Take charge of the spin before the reporter does; after all, she is someone who's seeking more of a sensational or amusing headline than your analysis of an issue.

When Janice Weinman spoke at the AAUW convention in 1997, she outlined the work that members had to do when the event was over and they returned home:

First, we will continue to act as a conscience and a voice for girls and for women. Secondly, we will serve as a resource for our supporters . . . . And third, we will become more efficient and responsive so that we can better serve our members in every facet of their lives.

Her logical presentation outlined the steps involved and helped listeners follow her key points. She then went on to explain each point more thoroughly with examples of how all this will happen.

This is important because leaders build scenarios for their listeners. Journalist Liz Carpenter advises: "Start with the past, put the meat in the middle, and wave the flag at the end." Think about your favorite topic. What's the history and background of the problem? What's the substance of your idea? This is where you spend most of your allotted time. How, at the end of your talk, can you create a sense of community to rally the troops? Carpenter's strategy is to pack an emotional punch at the close without sacrificing substance, or "the meat."

Your delivery must convey to the audience that you are confident about your intellect. When you propose a plan of action to your audience, you consider the big picture and develop strategies from there. You won't, however, ignore the details of carrying out your plan, and the human costs involved in production and service delivery. You consider what is in the common good when you propose action. Your argument must be based on logical reasoning and provide current information. Men don't have an edge on reason. Judging from the way in which male leaders have historically rationalized political actions that were impulsive, expedient, self-serving, and often violent, some would argue that women are more reasonable than men.

Shifting from the Subjective to the Strategic

If the audience is skeptical about your credibility as the voice of authority, how do you address their concerns? We think of this as a "meta-level" of communication, and in some ways your strategy for achieving credibility is more important than your topic. You can experiment with the following four communication strategies that include being direct, being logical, being specific, and watching the tendency to disclose too much too soon that is too personal.

First, if you propose action, be direct about your proposal in a way that is easy to understand; for example:

◆ *"What we need to do now is to . . . . If not, there are going to be three predictable consequences."*

Second, be logical in the way you present arguments and stay focused on your topic; for example:

◆ *"When we discuss the impact of practices that produce pollution, we must consider air, land, as well as water . . . . "*

Third, be specific about your expertise and avoid modesty; for example,

◆ *"I've spent two years in the field working with 300 clients (patients, students, researchers, et al) and have learned five lessons that saved us millions."*

Fourth, use just the right amount of self-disclosure to make a point but not so much that you become self-indulgent. Self-disclosure can be a powerful way to connect with your audience; for example:

◆ *"I am a cancer survivor. At first, I was devastated by the news. While I certainly wouldn't recommend choosing to have cancer, I feel that—ironically—I'm a better person and have a richer life as a result. Today I'll share three lessons I've learned from surviving cancer."*

You may be tempted to feel sorry for yourself in having to think on several tracks at the same time: organizing your ideas, relating to the audience, and establishing credibility. It's like that old joke about Fred Astaire and Ginger Rogers.[49] They both do the same steps but she dances backwards in high heels. Double standards, double bind. With a clear strategy to help you gain credibility, however, you have the tools to break the tie that binds.

Let's analyze the key ingredients that can ensure your credibility as a leader:

First, leaders have access to resources and networks. Can you deliver on the promises you'll make? To address the audience's concern about whether you have access to resources and networks, ask yourself:

◆ *How would this audience define "resources?" How would they define "networks?"*

◆ *What resources and networks do I bring to the table?*

Resources aren't just measured in wealth. They can include people, access to the media, and your ability to get out the voters. They can be the groups, associations, church, or temple to which you belong. Think about your resources and networks beforehand because they demonstrate to the audience that you have power and influence.

Second, leaders must be made of tough stuff. The audience is wondering if you can handle conflicts and tough negotiations. Make a list of a few examples to demonstrate that you have a proven track record. Select one and brag to you friends. Do any of these situations apply to you?

☐ *When did I negotiate an important deal that created profit for the company?*

☐ *When did I step in to solve a problem, saving the organization time, money, and grief?*

☐ *When did I remain cool and levelheaded when everyone else in the group—both men and women— wanted to sweep a conflict under the rug?*

☐ *When did I find a way to resolve a messy, awkward, embarrassing, or vulnerable situation with a customer, member, vendor, or investor?*

Find examples to demonstrate that you're a proven leader. You aren't easily swayed but, rather, you can evaluate the pros and cons and help groups find the best solutions.

Third, leaders need to stay focused and not be manipulated by their feelings. Men are perceived to be more in control of their feelings than women are. Ask yourself:

☐ *What examples can I give of times when I had to make those tough decisions that would be hard for any mortal?*

☐ *When did I demonstrate that I could fire someone I liked, or hire someone I didn't like for the good of the organization?*

☐ *When did I survive a life-or-death or make-or-break situation because I stayed on task?*

When you present an emotional story, demonstrate that you have a point to make, not with a hidden agenda or a need to ventilate, castigate, or play the victim. Of course men have feelings and have been at the mercy of them, just as any human might, but the audience doesn't assume it's an issue that would impede their ability to be leaders, whether true or not. Interestingly, when men express emotions in public— even to excess—their emotionality is not seen as a demonstration of frailty. Women don't have the same option.

Fourth, leaders keep the big picture in mind and don't get lost in the details. For centuries, women have been in charge of the details of domestic life and the details of the workplace. To make sure that you are seen as a big picture thinker who is logical and systematic, your presentation must begin with a statement of your vision and an action plan. Outline your proposal in terms of the following points:

◆ *What is the ideal future scenario?*

◆ *Why is my proposal a win-win solution?*

◆ *What are the broad general strategies that will allow us to realize this vision?*

◆ *What will I do to ensure that we achieve this vision?*

The leader relies on others to actually implement the plans but, as a visionary, she focuses on the desired end point.

Why not predict tough questions in advance and be ready with a brief answer? Ask yourself:

☐ *Where am I vulnerable to criticism or a challenge?*

☐ *Might I be perceived as having a conflict of interest or a hidden agenda?*

☐ *What statistics are needed to strengthen my argument?*

No one likes confrontation or conflict, but politicians, activists, and advocates we interviewed are accustomed to being on the spot and want the upper hand. Next time you watch a press conference, notice how the effective speaker turns the tough questions around to her advantage by getting back to her key points and staying on message.

Fifth, leaders aren't modest. Men describe their success as being due to ability, women to a bout of good luck, that feminine modesty thing again. Was it a round of good luck that got you where you are today? Of course not. It's a no-brainer.

You have worked hard to make your way to the podium. The audience needs to know quite clearly that you were not "discovered" the day of the presentation; rather, your sustained high level of performance and ability led you to the podium. You know your stuff, and want to bring people together to increase mutual success. Your skills and knowledge base are critical to your leadership capacities. When you lead the group forward, it will be through your expertise and strategic thinking, not through mercurial turbulence, fate, or what used to be described as women's manipulative charms.

The audience wonders if you're going to be dabbling in leadership. Are you someone who is in for the long haul, or a dilettante who'll leave the leadership role for home and hearth when her biological clock goes off? These are not questions that men have to answer, but let's answer those questions—and the underlying concerns—before they are asked. Regardless of your topic, and however you weave it in, your overarching meta-message is: "I am a capable, credible leader who can juggle many roles."

To that concern, we reply that women want the same choices that men have, whether or not they choose to be a parent. Why not make it clear that you can play many roles in life? You want that raise, you want to win the election, or you want to improve your community—period.

Do you look and sound like a leader? The anecdotes you share, the examples you give, the logical organization of your key points are strategies to address any concerns that the audience might have about your capacity to be a leader based on the stereotypes that overly value masculine traits and devalue feminine traits. Prepare yourself to deliver your message by shifting your strategies to a more assertive style that demonstrates your capacity for leadership, and you will dare to be bold.

Applying Your Conversational Strengths to the Formal Presentation

Good conversation is interactive and involves give-and-take, listening, and then responding to another person. In this social role, women tend to test the waters before they take the plunge and a position, particularly on a controversial topic. You know communication is a two-way street. You want to relate. You're interested in someone other than yourself. You know how to react and find common ground. Of course you can do that. But being a bold communicator who tells people—in public settings—what they should do or how they should think is a new role for many women.

Actually, we don't have much of a choice. Public speaking is historically structured as a monologue, not a dialogue. What people expect from a presentation or speech is a "talking-at" structure. The audience is quiet, with eyes and ears focused on the speaker, who is expected to have a strong personality and a point of view. After all, the speaker's role *per se* requires an assertive expression of opinion. We expect a male public speaker to have a position, a vantage point for seeing the world, and solutions for the problem at hand. Being assertive comes with the public speaker's territory. You need to take the reins. But to stay on the horse you need to make sure that you and your audience are moving in the same direction.

If you outline your key points in advance, you'll move forward in a logical manner. Number your points; use transition words such as "first" . . . "second" . . . , and "third." Begin with a reference to "what we all know to be true" and "what we all want . . . " and keep referring to the big picture as you make your way across the minefields. Showing the audience your logical mind is your hidden agenda. Taking an impulsive tangent is not an option when the audience is watching for signs that you might be scatterbrained. Instead, keep your eye on the big picture, as all good leaders do.

LESSON
*Shift from a subjective to a bold, strategic approach
in planning your presentation.*

CHAPTER 8

Flawless Delivery

She is so familiar with the ideas that [she can read] and also look up and connect with her audience with perfect inflection. She's someone with flawless delivery. . . In her swearing-in ceremony, there were over 1,000 people in the room, and you could hear a pin drop.

> — Ida Castro describing Alexis Herman,
> Former Secretary of Labor

The road to flawless delivery begins with preparing your mind and body. There is no formula, no magic bullet for feeling confident at the podium.

Find Ways to Relax

Starting is the hard part. Writers dread facing that first sheet of blank white paper. Speakers who dread facing an audience often experience heart palpitations, sweaty palms, lightheadedness, and fear of losing their memory—and their lunch—at the podium. Luckily, speakers have offered a range of suggestions for taking control of the jitters.

Prime Minister Winston Churchill, the speaker who inspired millions to fight an unpopular war, managed his anxiety by imagining the audience (probably members of Parliament) sitting in their underwear. That's a mental picture that will make you relax and remind you that the audience members are only human—just like you.

The audience wants you, the speaker, to succeed. After all, if the speaker fails, listeners have wasted their time. Audience members have been known to rationalize the mediocre performance of a speaker for just this reason. Find that friendly face, and begin there.

Being relaxed when you speak does involve breathing easily, so why not think of speaking—at least metaphorically—as an athletic event? Betsy Myers warms up for her presentations the way athletes do. She stretches herself before delivering a major conference presentation by giving dozens of smaller presentations. With each presentation, she learns something that gives her new ideas and modifies her outline until the big day. She observes other speakers to learn why they succeeded or failed and experiments with new techniques to hone her own skills. In general, she learns more about the psychology of speaking from her own practice as well as role models, which in turn lessens her own anxiety.

Warm Up Your Audience

Speaker Liz Carpenter believes you need to warm up the *audience*. She begins slowly by acknowledging them and whatever it is that they have in common. Are they women firefighters? Are they members of the chamber of commerce? She's faced them both. Be sure you know your audience's particular issues, values, and interests, or you may step into a minefield. A joke in poor taste, a reference to an opposing political party, or a remark about a particular lifestyle may seem harmless to you but might be seen as irreverent and disrespectful by audience members. Once this happens, your credibility may be squashed. Audiences will forgive your limitations if they feel you've cared enough to do your homework.

Demonstrate that you want to be there. Susan Lowell

Butler believes that a good speaker will show that she is interested in a particular group or audience.

In order to speak about what is relevant to that audience, make contact with that audience. Convey that you want to be there. Use your adrenaline. Don't do it if you don't want to be there. If you're miserable and you hate them, it will show. Trust me on that.

Grounded, or On the Ledge with an Edge?

Your voice is also a reflection of your confidence. Women's voices—in terms of tone and quality—can be as varied and unique as an individual fingerprint. We no longer need to feel limited by one style that is deemed appropriate for a feminine voice. Loud, soft, husky, or lyrical, we can vary our voices so as to express our unique personalities and emphasize the points we make by changing volume and breathing. But we can generalize about one thing: leaders don't whisper, not if they want to be seen and heard.

For women, however, it's a fine line between whispering and what the audience may perceive as shouting. For instance, Los Angeles County Supervisor Gloria Molina is often described by critics as "having an edge," but this may well reflect the different standard for men and women. Susan Lowell Butler believes that kind of comment occurs when women begin to get too effective:

I am rarely strident, but I can be. I can have the type of voice that can etch glass. As a former public school teacher, you get that way. But I tend to be a little softer now.

According to Liz Carpenter, Gloria Steinem has a "slow, modulated voice, as soft as Eleanor Roosevelt's." Her voice is easy on the ears even when she presents radical ideas.

Marie Wilson knows that ideas about equality between men and women can be received well in some places but not others. When she speaks about "feminism" in a conservative environment, she can be perceived as strident regardless of her style or manner. "Sometimes," she adds, "your point of view is the issue." Your content might be well organized and style of delivery could be perfect but you still would be ineffective because the audience's values and attitudes conflict with yours and they tune you out.

Sex role socialization has narrowed women's choices about how a "feminine" woman should sound. But most important is the need to sound like a woman, not a little girl with a singsong voice and a rising inflection at the end of the sentence. You can hear this in "valley girl" talk, which is pervasive amongst teens. This was the old model for how women should sound.

The standards for how today's more assertive, straight-talking business and professional women should sound has changed. Today we are comfortable hearing a deeper voice in a lower register, typical of women newscasters. Listen to Connie Chung, Diane Sawyer, Cokie Roberts, and Jane Pauley on major networks, including CNN. What do you sound like on tape? Are you the voice of authority? Are people surprised when they meet you because you sound like a young girl on the phone? Is your voice congruent with the image you want to convey? If you modified the tone, quality, and pitch of your voice, you might have greater success being seen and heard. Practicing these changes with a tape recorder can help, and it's easier than you might think, once you are willing to become your own coach.

Of course you want feel confident about making your points with just the right emphasis. Your success in communicating your key points depends primarily on how you can vary the volume, rate of speech, and pitch. Your inflection can rise, indicating a question or tentativeness, or your inflection can fall, emphasizing a statement. We think most vocal problems can be easily corrected once you become aware of how you sound to others. Using a small tape recorder, read aloud today's Op Ed piece in the local paper. You'll quickly hear the places you need to make adjustments in volume, pitch, inflection, or pace.

To test your ability to emphasize your points, read the sentence below as if it were a question with an upward inflection:

"For company morale, we really need an annual dinner (?)"

Then reread the sentence as a declarative statement.

"Yes, for company morale, we really need an annual dinner!"

Your Voice Is Your Instrument

In getting people excited about your proposal, you'll want to highlight the most shocking, surprising, amazing facts you want people to remember. Without a yellow highlighter, you only have your voice or the dramatic pause for emphasis. Make a list of the steps in resolving a problem that people can relate to. Say the first step out loud. Take a deep breath. Pause, and count to three. The silence between your key points—as indicated below by the word "breathe"—allows the listener to digest the information. To evaluate your voice, read the following sentences out loud into a tape recorder, and emphasize the key point in each by pausing before each key point:

◆ Last year's NASDAQ investment **went up** (breathe) **25 percent** today.

◆ Infant mortality in poor neighborhoods is up (breathe) **10 percent** over last year's.

- Test scores in the inner city schools are **up five points** (breathe) since last year.

- Global warming is no joke. Consider that the **20 percent ice melt rate** in Alaska has caused (breathe) **flooding and homelessness** in the Plains states.

- The number of languages spoken in the Ballard elementary school is up to (breathe) **forty-eight languages.**

Write your own sentences to make it more relevant, underline the key words, and tape yourself again. Play back the tape and listen to the sound of your voice. Try it again, varying the volume, rate, and pitch until you're satisfied that you've adequately emphasized your points.

Hit the Ground Running

As a news reporter, Liz Carpenter learned from the old *New York Daily News* rule of thumb to "hit them in the head with the lead." After all, the readers may never make it to the second paragraph. Use the same axiom in speaking. Get to the point. Once you're off and running, your confidence and authoritative tone will make the audience want to follow. By then, your breathing will have become regular again.

Susan Butler used the formal rules of speaking to guide her:

You have thirty seconds to get the group's attention— maybe fifteen—so you had better find a way to quickly get a hold of your audience.

A shocking quote, a statistic, or a stunning visual aid can be used effectively to send the message: "I'm the voice of authority, I'm the expert, and I mean business, so listen up." Women tend to begin with prefaces or apologies but you know better so, ba-da-bing! If you have any self-doubts, keep them to yourself. Once you dive straight on in, you'll swim, rather than sink. For example, here is an effective way to start your presentation about a teen.

> *Decreased teen violence and increased academic achievement are just two reasons why our community should support free after-school music and drama program at our high school. Let me address each of those two benefits. First . . .*

Gaining the audience's confidence means that a woman must develop her point as someone with the voice of authority, a take-charge action-oriented type of person. That might sound like this:

> *Our city's mass transit system is **no longer safe**. **Fifty-six percent** of the city's population has lost confidence in the system. Congestion on the freeways is **at an all-time high,** according to the* Times. *As treasurer of the downtown association whose neighborhood is most affected, I propose **a three-step plan** to attack our problems. This plan will take one year to implement but there are no **additional tax revenues,** and the plan provides **safe travel for every city resident.***

Focus Yourself and Focus Your Listeners

It's easy to let your nervousness derail you. Veteran political speaker Liz Carpenter uses notes to make sure she stays on track. She writes, "Slow down!" reminders in the margins of her outline because her tendency is to speak too fast. Since many of her speeches have been recycled over the past fifty years, she certainly knows the key points but still wants those notes in front of her as a security blanket, "right down there where I can get to them." Better to be safe than sorry. If you should feel lost, notes in the margin can help you get back to your next point.

No one knows everything that can be known about a

subject, so focus on one particular topic where you feel most prepared. You want to present your ideas logically so that the audience can easily follow along. One way is to frame your presentation as a story with a beginning, middle, and an end. The "plot" moves forward toward a resolution. The "characters" in your story—that is, the people involved—are clearly defined. Just as in a good story, nothing is extraneous. Everything fits together to create tension and maintain interest. In your presentation, you have a solution to a problem or a proposal to make. Each point you make is going to lead the audience to agree with you and see the situation from a new point of view—yours. In your outline, you will move through your main points, including an example, a statistic, a quote, and/or a reason why the listeners should care about the issue.

Another way to organize your ideas is to imagine them as a series of sheets that you're hanging on a clothesline. Each sheet is lined up in a row, and you pin them up one at a time. They reach across the line until all the bedding is in plain view. In your presentation, imagine each point as if it were a sheet and you're making your case, the way you might make your bed. However you imagine the component parts of your presentation, they need to fit together logically so that the audience can see the whole picture and appreciate your ability to differentiate between extraneous and necessary information. After all, you're the expert.

How do you make sure that your audience remembers your key points? Telling and remembering are two different things. Gloria Steinem delivered a commencement speech at Tufts University in 1987. She told the crowd that she didn't remember one thing from the speech given by her cleverly organized commencement speaker when she graduated and wanted to be very clear about her "Thoughts" about "what I know now that I wish I'd known then," by enumerating them as Thought Number One, Thought Number Two, Thought Number Three, and so on. We liked—Thought Three— "choosing character over intelligence in a friend" (or a candidate) and—Thought Six—"the value to men of combining work and family life for the pleasure and rewards of being a whole human being. More recently, she used a similar approach in a speech to a primarily college-aged group in Santa Barbara, California, prior to Election Day, November 7, 2000. Steinem presented "The top ten reasons not to vote for Ralph Nader." By enumerating her main points, the audience found it easy to follow her logic, and she kept us focused throughout her presentation.

In Your Own Words

Successful speakers use everyday language. It's tempting to use scientific or technical jargon, particularly if you're trying to score points with a mainly male audience. But the brief description of the problem as a story or a picture conveys more than any acronym or statistic. *"We spend more money sending boys to jail than we do sending boys to Yale,"* said Jesse Jackson, the master of rhyme. Easy to say but hard to forget. Memorable speakers use clear and powerful language. When she was the keynote speaker delivering the commencement address at Harvard University, Barbara Jordan demonstrated the use of simple language when she said:

> *What the people want is simple. They want an America as good as its promise.*[50]

Journalist Liz Carpenter thinks that academic language is dull and lifeless; she's been a professional speaker for most of her life, so she should know. If your audience is mixed and there are technical professionals, university professors, or specialists listening to you, you may want to make your point once for the academy and once again for the ordinary folks. A complicated point is worth repeating and approaching from different angles. If you make your point in a memorable way, you're more likely to be quoted. Can you think of a memorable sentence you'd like reporters to use when they quote you speaking about your favorite topic?

Marie Wilson of the Ms. Foundation believes that audiences are sincerely curious to hear how women from diverse backgrounds are putting their lives together these days. For instance, how do women juggle a complex array of roles? Are you a member of "the multitasking sandwich-generation" juggling the needs of young children with the needs of aging parents? Are you returning to school mid-life, or juggling dual careers while trying to beat the biological clock? Are you negotiating the needs of everyone in today's blended families while running your business? You have new stories to tell about the costliness of that experience, both in economic as well as psychological terms. Don't silence yourself from describing what it's like to juggle many roles; if it fits into your presentation, feel free to speak from your own experience.

Effective speakers may use their regional dialects as a way to pull the audience into their unique story. Whether you're from the south, north, east, or west, however, there are common social issues that we can all relate to. Excerpts from regional folk tales, films, novels, and historical events from your part of the world can spice up your presentation and make it truly unique. If you can articulate common concerns that we all share, in spite of your unique background, you will have helped listeners to feel connected to the big picture and larger societal trends.

Prepare for the Unexpected

So you figured out your strategy, you know how to relate to the audience, and you've got stories to back up your hard-hitting points. Even so, sometimes circumstances prevail that are out of your control, and you find yourself unprepared. For example, what if the person who writes the press release decides to get creative with the title of your talk, or an unexpected organizational or political crisis makes your specific topic suddenly irrelevant?

Butler recalls:

I've been told whole different things that I was going to talk about and then, "Big bang! Hello!" and "Surprise!" What you don't do is blame the person who invited you to speak in that particular public setting. Frankly, I've never been invited to speak on "The Power of Public Education" and gotten there and been told that I had to speak on quantum physics.

Sometimes Murphy's Law prevails and the worst does happen. The microphone has static and the air-conditioning fails. The longwinded speaker prior to you on the agenda cuts into half of your time. In situations when everything that can go wrong does, it's best to maintain a perspective. Shortly after Professor Carol Nadelson, M.D., was elected the first female president of the American Association of Psychiatrists, she attended a major international meeting where presidents of the national associations were being asked to say a few words of greeting.

The chairman asked the AAP's previous president to speak, but he declined, saying that Dr. Nadelson was now the president, but, as people were asked to come up to the podium, when her turn would have come, the lights went out—as it if were the end of the program. "I

had a split second to decide what to do; was I going to
ignore it ... or confront it? I went up to the microphone,
on the stage, in the dark, and I made some welcoming
remarks.[51]

Men in the audience didn't really understand what had
happened, including the man who turned out the lights,
although she soon learned that the other women in the room
had realized what had happened. Without being able to see
anyone's response, she had to make a choice. Though she
couldn't be seen, she could be heard. The only way to
demonstrate that she was in charge was through her voice
and ability to be articulate. Dr. Nadelson went on with her
presentation, making the best of a bad situation. If you had
been in her shoes, what would you have done?

The more you speak to groups, the more you'll learn that
these kinds of problems are more the norm than the exception. Above all, remain flexible and remember what you set
out to accomplish. Accommodate the group's timeframe.
The interviews we conducted indicate that there are four
strategies to cope with a potential disaster:

+ If you have to cut your speech, trim the fat off the
  presentation but leave the heart.

+ Prepare handouts in advance with the facts that you
  no longer have time to discuss in person.

+ Be available during the break to speak with people
  informally.

+ Ask the organization to publish the key points of your
  talk in their newsletter.

Above all, when the unexpected happens, convey confidence in your competence. Don't become overly emotional
or illogical or you may fit the sexist stereotype of women as
hysterical creatures who fall apart when things go wrong.
Focus on the importance of getting your message out to this

particular audience in whatever time is available, and make the best of the situation. How you handle the unexpected disaster is part of your message.

Delivering a presentation at a conference event can be a challenge. You need to know who comes before and after you speak. Betsy Myers makes sure she knows where she stands in the lineup. She analyzes the context, asking:

- ☐ *Am I scheduled to speak after lunch, when people are lethargic?*

- ☐ *Am I the opening speaker, and therefore the one who is expected to energize the crowd and give people a sense of what's ahead?*

- ☐ *Am I the final speaker who closes the proceedings and has a chance to leave the group with something really memorable?*

Each slot has certain opportunities and minefields. This is where being a strategic thinker comes into play: if you need to shorten your remarks, what key points can you eliminate, and what are the essential key points that you must convey?

Relating to rude audiences can be tough. Butler faced another difficult audience when she was quite new as the NEA Communications Director. She was invited to address the business roundtable at the National Chamber of Commerce about what public education teachers really want.

I was quite nervous . . . grim as death, and didn't feel quite comfortable in my job. As a result, they cleaned my clock. They said things like, "Well, honey, you say that teachers need more money. Well, I don't think they work real hard. What's your answer to that?" I got through the speech but we were not communicating, to say the least. And I certainly did not blow them away with brilliance.

Impact of Your Delivery

Clearly, if you achieve your purpose, you've made an impact. You raise money for a campaign. You get support for your proposal. You win the election. Your legislation is passed. You get people in the audience to take action. One of the most difficult roles for most women to take on is to ask for money. Ms. Foundation Director Marie Wilson says that "if you love what you do, then you're bold about asking other people to contribute to it." In this way, women's speaking style is often more process-oriented than men's:

> *It's not like making a pitch. . . . it's not what you do at the very end that gets people to give . . . it's building a relationship with the audience, so that they trust what you're saying, that what you're wanting them to put their resources into is as powerful . . . and important as you say it is.*

CEO Laura Groppe wants to motivate venture capitalists to invest in her company, Girl Games, Inc. She'd enjoy having women endorse her company but this isn't easy because:

> *This is the first generation of women with pocket change they've earned themselves. I learn to talk with and listen to women about their concerns, and we figure out a way to accommodate their capacity to take risks.*

She knows she's succeeded as a motivational speaker if the checks start arriving.

Kathleen Drennan, chair for the Advancement of Women's Health, was the president and CEO of her company, one which sponsored clinical trials. She is clear that public speaking skills made an impact on the public and were critical to her corporate success.

My public speaking skills got us known and won our reputation. People identified the company with me, they liked me, liked what I was saying, and therefore liked the company. This whole public speaking thing was phenomenal. Being seen and heard is exactly what built my reputation and business.

As you gain speaking experience, you'll come to know when you're relating to the audience and how to pace yourself. Speaker Ida Castro believes that you can tell when the audience is mesmerized and you've hit your peak.

A lot of people assume you shut up after you exhaust your points, wit, and jokes. In my opinion, you end the speech when everyone is mesmerized. Failure is overplaying your cards. Leave them wanting more.

Butler believes that there are five indicators of speaker success, probably in this order:

- ◆ People come up to you (after your presentation) and hang around.
- ◆ People begin to quote you within the organization and to the press.
- ◆ Your reputation begins to spread and you're asked to speak at other conferences.
- ◆ The speaking engagement involves a paid fee.
- ◆ Your public speaking helps to get the bill passed or get the policy changed.

Speaker Ann Stone has different criteria. She knows that she made an impact when she:

- ◆ wins a political debate.
- ◆ receives top evaluations when she speaks at conferences.

In general, you know you've succeeded in taking your ideas public when you get press coverage and, as they say, one thing leads to another. Today's presentation to your staff could lead to a board of trustees meeting, and then to an industry-wide conference, with reporters not far behind.

Consider your own criteria for success. *How will you know you've made an impact? Do you want to change attitudes or behavior? Would you define success as any of the following outcomes?*

- ☐ *You won the election.*
- ☐ *You helped to avert a strike.*
- ☐ *Your proposed policy is approved and funded.*
- ☐ *You raised awareness of issues that were being neglected.*
- ☐ *You sold a new product or service.*
- ☐ *People invested in your company.*
- ☐ *You built team spirit.*

Write down your exact goal on an index card when you prepare your next presentation. Make it short and simple. Keep this card in front of you as you organize your remarks. For some women speakers, making contact with the audience is the best reward. Their primary purpose is to cultivate political or business relationships. Others need to make an impact and achieve an specific goal.

Prepare for the Possibility of Confrontation

It's human nature to resist change. People are invested in keeping things "the-way-they-were," and they can get downright hostile when you propose something new. Historical and contemporary role models—including the women we present in this book—demonstrate that it is possible to tolerate emotional responses or negativity without losing your cool.

In fact, tough questions are inevitable if you are championing a controversial cause or proposing that a group change its organizational direction. You may find that someone in the group is confrontational during the Q and A, challenging the accuracy or currency of your information and your credibility as an expert. *It's nothing personal but will you take it personally? Will you break?* Not if you've prepared yourself thoroughly by knowing your subject matter, knowing your position, and knowing your audience. Use your imagination to predict the worst thing that might happen. Play out different scenarios beforehand so you are ready for anything, including the courage to say, "I need to think about that and get back to you." You'll want to be seen and heard as a woman who is prepared for the tough questions, as all good leaders are.

LESSON
*A woman speaker can cultivate flawless delivery by
preparing herself to sound like leader and
choosing to make an impact.*

CHAPTER 9

Storytelling and Relating

What I have learned is that 95 percent of what you accomplish in life is because of relationships.
—Betsy Myers, Former Director of the
White House Office for Women

For most men, the act of speaking to another person one-on-one involves dominating the conversation. Talking at an audience for the purpose of conveying and "selling" their message is a more comfortable role. For women, speaking to an audience is a way of sharing their point of view with other people. Their purpose in speaking is more often to stimulate dialogue and discussion, not necessarily to convince the audience that they are right. Women enjoy public speaking more when they think of it as relating to the audience, as informally as if they were engaged in a conversation.

One of the primary ways that women relate to and learn from others is through exchanging and comparing stories in conversation. When the speaker needs to move beyond casual conversation in order to influence the group to adopt her point of view, she can still utilize storytelling strategies.

Women Excel at Storytelling

All of the speakers interviewed for this book believe that storytelling is a powerful tool, one that is an appropriate way to express ideas and feelings on important subjects, not just for cultivating friendships and workplace relationships. In earlier centuries, stories were used to explain the facts of life as well as how to function in assigned roles. Stories were used to explain cultural and religious traditions, childbearing, menses, menopause, birth, healing, food preparation, and household matters, as well as methods of planting and harvesting crops, church administration, and civic life.

"Telling stories is powerful," according to communications expert Susan Lowell Butler, who believes that:

> You can be stupid with a story, and you can bore everyone to death, but a personal *story that illustrates a point will always be most effective.*

Your stories about your own life are unique. No one can steal them or make them up or accuse you of idle gossip. What point would you like to make and which personal anecdote might help you make that point? Think about the most dramatic moments of your life and what you learned from a divorce, a bankruptcy, or the death of a loved one. Each one of those stories has the potential to move others in an emotional way that can be transformational. As a result of your storytelling abilities, the listeners may see everyday reality differently.

We use stories to talk about generational differences:

> My mother used the following Robert Browning quote in my sixth grade yearbook: "Be good sweet maid, and let who will be clever." For my mother, and the women of her generation, being good and sweet were the ultimate virtues. I learned later how much she had compromised her own dreams by being the good wife to someone who didn't share her interests. The day that she died was transformational for me. Soon after that I

began to speak up for women, and their right to pursue
big dreams of their own.

Stories can also bring us together in sharing anecdotes about cultural events that will transcend differences in our roles, ages, race, ethnicity, or sex. When these major events are traumatic for a group—or a nation—it can be cathartic for each of us to express our personal feelings about the event. For example, members of the sixties' generation often ask: *"Where were you when Kennedy was shot?",* *"when the Challenger exploded?" or "when Martin Luther King Jr. was assassinated?"* The equivalent question for Generation X might well be, *"What did you think was happening when you first saw those planes flying into the World Trade Center?"* Women might ask, *"Were you affected by watching Anita Hill give testimony against Clarence Thomas's confirmation to the Supreme Court?*

Establishing common ground is a tried and true method of beginning a presentation. Former Press Secretary Liz Carpenter believes you must tell your own story, tell it well, and not be timid about what you're saying, especially if you feel it's worth saying. We each have a personal story about the impact of those momentous events that is just waiting to be told. If you use your story to establish a common frame of reference with your audience and then move on to address your topic, your audience will be more inclined to listen and trust you.

At the August 2000 Democratic Convention, Hillary Clinton spoke about the work she did to support the foster care system and the need to see that neglected and abused foster children are being adopted into loving, permanent families. She gave a human face to their plight when she described one particular child called "Diana:"

. . . Just twelve years old, not much younger than

Chelsea at the time, she spent most of her life moving from house to house. She was so shy she could barely look up as she spoke of her longing for a home and family of her own. As I listened, I thought: "How can we let any child grow up in our country without a secure and loving home?"[52]

She then disclosed relevant personal information about her family:

I thought of what my own mother went through as a child, born to teenage parents who couldn't take care of her. When she was eight, she and her little sister were sent alone on a train across the country to stay with relatives. At fourteen, she went to work caring for a family's children. Her employer was a kind woman who saw her true worth and showed her what a loving family was really like.

Stories can also be used to inspire. Marie Wilson wants to change women donors' consciousness about philanthropy through their involvement in the fundraising development process. Historically, women haven't had access to discretionary money, but that situation is slowly changing. In her presentations, Wilson includes stories about how women have made a difference at every level of philanthropic giving. For instance, one young woman in Massachusetts raised money to build a school in Pakistan by organizing her schoolmates, albeit funding one classroom at a time. Her point was that even one very young woman could create monumental change by mobilizing other small donors.

By contrast, Wilson also tells a story to her audiences about an heiress whose family made their fortune in the garbage collection business. This is not your typical image of a Park Avenue type of heiress by any stretch of the imagination, which is why it's an interesting story. That young woman is now in the position to use some of her inheritance to create positive changes for others. Although increasing numbers of professional and businesswomen are also now financially independent and able to donate to foundations, they are still new to the world of philanthropy and don't yet understand the power they have to affect change with their resources. Told in an intimate, conversational manner as if sitting around the kitchen table, one woman to another, Wilson tells stories to redefine philanthropy as a woman's game. There are two messages here for her listeners: "Every one of us can find some spare change somewhere," and "At some time in our lives, we may inherit money, even from parents of modest means."

Celebrity speakers can be self-effacing and disclosing in order to appear more like members of the audience. At a May 1995 commencement address at Smith, Gloria Steinem told an amusing story about being a college student in a geology class:

> On a field trip, while everyone else was off looking at the cut-off meander curves of the Connecticut River, I was paying no attention whatsoever. Instead, I had found a giant turtle that had climbed out of the river, crawled up a dirt road, and was in the mud on the embankment of another road, seemingly about to crawl up on it and get squashed by a car. So being a good co-dependent with the world, I tugged and pushed and pulled until I managed to carry this huge, heavy, angry, snapping turtle off the embankment and down the road.

> I was just putting it back into the river when my geology professor arrived and said, "You know, that turtle probably spent a month crawling up that dirt road to lay its eggs in the mud by the side of the road and you've just put it back in the river." Well, I felt terrible. Only years later did I realize that this was the most impor-

*tant political lesson I learned, one that cautioned me
about the authoritarian impulse of both the right and
the left. The moral was: always ask the turtle.*[53]

College graduates in the audience connect with the story
immediately, thinking. "Oh, that could have been me."

CEO Laura Groppe believes that men operate more on
facts and less on emotions than women do. If you agree, then
your presentation to a male audience should emphasize the
facts and rely less on personal anecdotes and emotional stories.
Storytelling and personal anecdotes may be more effective
influence-strategies for motivating female audiences to take
action than male audiences because it is the way women typically communicate with one another in everyday life. Groppe
integrates both techniques, depending on her audience.

In her mid-thirties, Groppe defies the conventional
image of a CEO. She tells audiences the story of how she
developed her business, Girl Games, Inc. After many setbacks
in her quest to find venture capitalists who would invest in
her business, she spent all her money and time flying around
the country doing product demos to Girl Scouts, as well as
through direct mail. Finally, her product began to sell in
computer stores.

One day in a CompUSA store demo, she finally saw
tremendous success and described it to her audience:

*I have this whole spazzy of girls in front of me who
won't put the thing down. Their mothers finally have to
buy hoards of products just to get them out of the store.
This little twelve-year-old girl comes up to me afterward and tugs on my skirt, looks up at me, and says, "I
just wanted to thank you. I've never had anything to
play with. My little brother is always on the computer
and just because you have started this company, I now*

have something to look forward to . . . . " And these stories happen to me all the time.[54]

The feedback from this one little girl made tears come to Groppe's eyes because it confirmed that her vision for Girl Games, Inc. had finally become a reality. She confides to her audience that, originally, her business was merely a dream, something she initially drew up on a piece of paper not even knowing how to build the software program. Listening to Groppe's story, the audience members are encouraged to follow their dreams. The moral of her story is " she can do it, maybe I can, too."

From twenty years of traveling to conferences and programs with Gloria Steinem, Marie Wilson has used the same anecdotes about women's outrageous acts—like nailing underwear to the wall—time and again. She laughs about hearing Gloria Steinem tell one of her favorite stories over and over again:

> *Gloria's brilliance is that she understands how many times a message has to be communicated for it to sink in. When I first started traveling with her, I wondered why she repeated certain stories and phrases. I finally understood what she knew that I needed to learn: Important ideas need to be repeated again and again. Now I do the same thing.*

Some personal stories bear repeating because they make an important point and you realize that they are guaranteed to score with an audience; in fact, these stories can become your trademark. Find a story that works with a certain group or audience, and tell it often. Just as a good sherry gets better with age, some stories bear retelling on special occasions, reunions, anniversaries, and commencements. Do you have a story to tell about yourself that people always enjoy? So, maybe it's not going to be "Eureka! And then I found the cure for cancer," Maybe you'll share something like, "I was so exhausted from lack of sleep I was sure I'd leave the baby on the bus!" Working parents can all relate. Everyone of us has had our splendid moments of epiphany and other times when we feel defeat and despair. What can **you** reveal about yourself through a poignant story that your audience will relate to?

Stories need to be relevant to your main message in establishing your credibility. Stories for their own sake that provide an opportunity to ventilate won't help you much. Stories about other people must contain accurate information and help you make your point so as not to derail you. Given those ancient stereotypes about women and their propensity for "gossip," you'll want to be especially accurate in mentioning names, dates, and places. At all costs, avoid the four horsemen of the apocalypse: rumor, gossip, hearsay, and innuendo. The grapevine feeds on misinformation, and you'll regret it in the morning when you have to eat your words.

Relationship and Contact

Susan Lowell Butler believes that the audience is open to a relationship. They'd rather leave saying, "What a great speaker!"

> *People need to be reassured that they're going to have a good experience with you. That's what you focus on in the beginning. . . . Public speaking is about relating to others. Just as in conversation, you want to make contact and have a future relationship. You're opening up to a series of contacts that you make. You don't have to be a show horse. You just have to want to be there and you have to be on top of the game.*

Janice Weinman believes that political action and who you are as a person is part of the same story.

Communicating about yourself is a very important connector with an audience . . . it does validate the fact that the kind of personal *position that you take is relevant to your political position on an issue.*

Weinman identifies the issues that her audiences care about, not just the ones that she cares about. She then indicates possible solutions that might work and how the audience members might get more involved in the political process. She makes that connection through self-disclosure and building rapport with the audience.

Women are in the relationship business. Recent research informs us that women conduct their lives through a web of relationships. Need advice? You probably call a friend or colleague to benefit from their networks. That's how women get practical information to help them find the best gynecologist, dentist, financial planner, mechanic, childcare program or therapist in town. Once you relate effectively to your listeners issues and interests, they will trust and quote you to others in their networks.

Building trust at the podium shouldn't be a problem, if women put their everyday relationship skills to work. That means knowing as much as possible about the audience beforehand.

◆ *What does the audience want and need? How can you meet their needs?*

◆ *Whom do you know in the group? Will they "dish," and how can that information help you connect with the group?*

◆ *What are three specific benefits from listening to you, your stories, your facts, and your proposals?*

Women like to relate to people who are likable and people who are like them. This isn't always possible. Select any of the following topics and outline the key points of one personal story you can share with an audience. Then practice with a group of friends:

- ☐ Career advancement in a sluggish economy
- ☐ Membership of The Sandwich Generation, caught in the middle
- ☐ Coping with the turbulent economy
- ☐ Raising children in a blended family
- ☐ Traveling well on a limited budget
- ☐ The stress of juggling many roles
- ☐ Pensions and planning for retirement post-Enron
- ☐ Teaching teens to make good choices in an MTV culture
- ☐ Ensuring that our children are safe in schools.

As someone who wants to continue to develop your competence as a speaker, you'll find it easier if you know something about the listeners. Check out the audience as carefully as if you were checking out a new friend. Your stories will build on those common threads. Make it clear that you share common perspective. *Are we all mid-life graduate students? Managers? Commuters? Is ours a nuclear family or are we single parents? Do we share common values like faith, hope, and charity?* Hillary Clinton made certain assumptions about the sympathies of her audience in the way that she spoke about the plight of foster children.

If giving a political presentation is part of your work or duty as a citizen, ask a few friends or trusted colleagues to join the audience. Find a few friendly faces—old or new—to focus on when you lose your adrenaline or if the debate gets contentious. Even if the presentation wasn't as successful as you had hoped it would be, use it as a learning experience and solicit feedback from your friends, including specific suggestions on how you might have more effectively related the topic to the audience. When the audience drifts, pull that special story out of your hat. When all else fails, *Alice in Wonderland*, *Sleeping Beauty*, and *Dr. Seuss* stories can be used as metaphors for what sometimes appears to be the madness in everyday life. What great myths and fairy tales apply to modern-day dilemmas? Your love of literature and a great quote can help you elevate your presentation to mythic proportions. Laura Groppe quotes poet Maya Angelou. *Do you have a file folder full of great book reviews, quotes, and your favorite poems?*

Nab the audience's attention by using a film excerpt to help tell your story and create an emotional response. Is there an excerpt from a film you can start with? Fast talking dames in movies of the forties showed us women with spunk and pluck. Many contemporary films like *Norma Rae*, *Nine-to-Five*, *The Candidate*, and *Frida* have images of lively, articulate, and creative women. Provocative films about the world of business, industry, and government are too numerous to mention. Which films appeal to you? How might you use an excerpt to begin your next presentation, and to make your point?

You can break down the architectural boundaries between yourself and your audience by sitting on the stage or walking through the audience, mike in hand, the way Liddy Dole did during her 2000 presidential campaign. Audiences like to rub elbows with the speaker in those few moments of access that provides a speaker with "celebrity" status. Proximity requires the listener to pay closer attention and feel as if she is truly engaged in a conversation. After all, the speaker might call on her or thrust the mike in front of her face for a comment asking "And what brings *you* here today?"

Most working women are familiar with PowerPoint technology and the bullet points can certainly help you feel confident that you won't forget your main points, but it can also become a barrier, a hindrance in relating to the audience. Former EEO Director Ida Castro has seen a corporate executive speak to a large group of female advocates only to lose them with dismal charts and a *Star Wars*-style presentation. Castro believes:

> *There are only so many numbers that an audience can absorb and hear in one sitting . . . the obligation and responsibility of the speaker is to convey the data that is essential and highlight the main points, either by contrast or by compliment. After I speak, people come up to me and ask for my stats [but] it wasn't really the stats I used, it was the context in which I presented them that gave significance and life to otherwise boring numbers.*

Women prefer active conversation to passive listening any day. This preference is probably what has led younger women to design new conferencing models that are more of a two-way dialogue and less of a one-way monologue. Businesswoman Laura Groppe described Lifetime Television's 1996 Women's Summit, which brought together accomplished women executives who are experts and specialists. They ignored the business-as-usual conference practice of offering "top-down" presentations of hard data delivered to passive listeners. Instead they used a bubble-up approach of interactive discussions, with summary presentations at the end by key speakers. Which do you prefer?

Relating to the audience requires that there be a balance of power between the speaker and the audience. Some people believe that the classical "talk-at" rhetorical approach needs to be challenged. For instance, journalist and feminist Gloria Steinem believes that you can "name" the separation between speaker and audience and ask the audience for their ideas regarding how to break down the barriers together. "That makes the audience already feel part of the process, not sitting there in judgment of you or just receiving whatever you say uncritically."[55]

Of course, if you really feel well prepared, you can limit your prepared remarks to just a few minutes and spend the bulk of your allotted time answering questions from the audience. Leaving your prepared outline is certainly risky; however, a skilled presenter who knows her subject inside and out is more willing to be spontaneous to achieve the excitement that comes from living in the moment.

Sometimes your presentation involves sharing the spotlight with celebrities or your heroes. Lowell Butler admits that when she was executive director of the National Women's Hall of Fame, she was too frightened to speak because of the prestigious women leaders who were sharing the stage with her and about to be inducted into the Women's Hall of Fame; these women included former Congresswoman Geraldine Ferraro, Native American leader Wilma Mankiller, former Congresswoman Shirley Chisholm and former Director of the Women's Bureau Esther Peterson.

The ceremony was held at Seneca Falls, the birthplace of the ERA Movement. In her opening remarks, Lowell Butler decided to paraphrase John Kennedy:

Never before in one place have there been assembled so many women of brilliance with so much to contribute except perhaps when Elizabeth Cady Stanton and Susan B. Anthony dined alone.

Butler recalls that the people in the audience were frozen in rapt attention during the next three-and-a-half hours, and that it seemed that "no one even breathed. One speaker after another came up and spun their stories afterward."

Whether you share a poignant family experience or disclose personal information, storytelling is a strategy for establishing common ground with your audience. The woman who uses stories effectively to make a point will be seen, heard, and remembered.

LESSON
Storytelling is an effective strategy for building a relationship with your audience.

CHAPTER 10

Women of Color

I have crossed over on the backs of Sojourner Truth and
Harriet Tubman and Fannie Lou Hamer and Madam C.J.
Walker. Because of them, I can now live the dream. I am the
seed of the free, and I know it. I intend to bear great fruit.[56]
—Oprah Winfrey

A democratic society deserves and demands that diverse
voices participate in policy debates and discussions. In
our multicultural and ethnically diverse world, it is critical to
our future that women of color* are seen and heard as leaders and spokespersons. The U.S. population has experienced
a substantial increase in the number of women who represent greater racial, ethnic, and cultural diversity, but will
these demographic shifts be considered when policy debates
and discussions occur? As long as we continue to see dispar-
ity in educational levels, household incomes, and leadership
positions for women in culturally diverse communities, it is
critical that women of color become vocal, taking positions
on policy matters that might remedy these imbalances.

When the speaker is a woman of color, she can add a

---

* Note: With appreciation to A. Lin Goodwin at Teachers College, Columbia
University for her definition of the term *of color* (Honoring Ways of Knowing,
Women's Educational Equity Act Newsletter, March 2000, p. 7). We use the term
to denote those individuals who are African American, Asian American, Latino,
and Native American, or who are not of European American descent, even while
we acknowledge that all human beings are, in actuality, people of color.

fresh, new voice to analyses of social, economic, educational, and political problems that affect everyone. Diversity is another word for enrichment; business leaders like Daisy Exposito believe that it is "the driving force in shaping today's America."[57] If you are a woman of color, you can discuss local, regional, and national problems—and the consequences of not solving a problem—with personal experiences, anecdotal material, and cultural examples that transcend statistics and might otherwise be ignored by male decision-makers.

A speaker's culturally or racially different life experiences and background can enhance, compliment, and expand the listener's comprehension of a problem. Finding good solutions to problems is critical at a time when social and economic problems are increasingly complex. Research by the State Department's Interagency Council on Women describes how shifting demographics have created new issues that are emerging for women of color of every age and circumstance throughout the world.[58] The diversity of women has become an increasingly complicated phenomenon due to the immigration of people from Latin America, as well as Southeast Asia and Eastern and Southern Europe. In general, women of color are significantly behind Caucasian women with regard to opportunities to work in nontraditional jobs, access to higher education and business advancement, and opportunities to enjoy a broader array of personal choices. Here are a few statistics:

- ◆ Nearly 25 percent of all American women are of color; ten million girls—or 8 percent of the total female population—were born outside the United States.

- ◆ Nearly 50 percent of Hispanic women and 80 percent of Asian-American women between the ages of eighteen and sixty-four are immigrants.

◆ There is an increase in the number of women without a fundamental knowledge of English. Spanish is the first language for most of the four million women—or 3 percent of all U.S. women—who live in linguistic isolation where no one over the age of thirteen speaks English fluently. (As referenced in the Appendix, page 233 and footnote 108.)

Who will represent the needs of culturally and racially diverse women when broad social policy decisions are made?[59]

Women in general, and women of color in particular, have been invisible as a result of the institutionalization of power in patriarchal societies. As diverse women expand upon the traditional roles to include new social, occupational, professional, and political roles, it is appropriate that they speak up in a range of public settings and, when they do, succeed as public speakers. This is no simple assignment. First, white men have traditionally been seen and heard as the voice of authority. Second, nonverbal communication is critically important to a speaker's effectiveness and many ethnic and cultural groups do not encourage or allow (as the case may be) girls and women to make eye contact, use broad gestures, or argue and debate. Women who have grown up within these cultural traditions that inhibit assertive communication will find public speaking particularly difficult because it requires them to violate those traditions and "feminine" norms. However, there are eloquent and articulate women of color who have learned to bridge the culture gaps that exist between them and their audience.

Why Women of Color Need to Speak Up

As a general rule, the men in minority communities are maintaining leadership positions and crafting policy. In many instances, the very organizations that represent our racial and ethnic communities, including our public educational institutions, consistently promote men over women. Lisa Sullivan, community activist, founder and president of LISTEN Inc., lends her observations about the African American community: ". . . for a long time in our community the women organized, and the men led. Now Black women who historically have done the organizing are crossing over into leadership."[60] One way that women can become more visible in their organizations is to develop their power as public speakers.

If you seek leadership, your position outside the system as a woman of color can be reframed as positive. The outsider asks questions that insiders may wish to avoid. For example, Thomasine Parott was discouraged with the way her union was run: "the same old way by the same old people and their friends and relatives." She started going to the meetings but understood very little about what was going on. She began to raise questions and ask for clarification of the issues, stirring up the interest of other employees as well as her own. Another union member commented on Parott's election as the union's first Black and female vice president:

I didn't really know her, but heard about her and that she would stand up to The Man. I found out her stuff was honest . . . . That's what made me vote for her . . . . Some people won't rock the boat, but she will and if everybody falls off, if there's nothing left but wind in her sail, she'll stand tall.[61]

Speaking can reflect every level of activism, from advocating for civil rights to communicating families' and neighbors' concerns to city councils. Success can happen when activists organize effectively to document and present problems to school board officials, as Padres Unidos did in Colorado. Dolores Obregon, a soft-spoken, middle-aged mother of five recalls:

Like so many others, I used to feel uncomfortable about standing up to a teacher or principal. I thought they were the educated ones who knew best. Since I got involved with Padres, I realized that I know what's best for my children.[62]

Liberal groups fight for their rights from the top down. For example, breaking through "the glass ceiling" may be very important to women seeking managerial success on the top floors of corporate America or in their professional life. This is not an important issue for many women of color, however, because they are supporting their families on minimum wage or through temporary and/or part-time jobs with no benefits. Grass-roots activists like Dolores C. Huerta must fight for the issues from the bottom up. The mother of eleven children, Dolores Huerta is the co-founder and first vice president emeritus of the United Farm Workers of America, AFL-CIO. Who will speak for poor women in organizations like the UFW if women like Dolores Huerta with similar experiences don't speak up to represent them?

Even where there is access, there is not necessarily success. "Doors are open, but minds are closed," reports Pamela Newkirk in an article in the *Washington Post.*[63] Newkirk's description of the challenges of Black journalists in a majority white media world also reflects the depth of challenge that women of color face even after they have climbed up a rung or two on the corporate ladder or achieved community leadership and, as a result, often find themselves onstage at the podium. The general public often credits those who are quoted in the media as being "experts." Whether they are or not, it is important that more women in general, and women of color in particular, ultimately become spokespersons, advocates, and experts. Think you can hide in the back row?

Not if you are trying to change social policy at the local level, need to raise money for candidates or your own campaign, influence people to join coalitions, and/or mobilize neighbors to attend city council meetings—all of which require effective public speaking. Leaders learn to *seize* opportunities to speak up at forums and commission hearings, participate in task forces and ad hoc committees, solicit media interviews, and contribute to local, national, and international policy debates. Success in local politics can be addictive, and a talented speaker can be quickly catapulted into state and national leadership roles.

In *Lessons from Gifted Women of Color*, researcher Margie Kitano notes that women of color tend to employ a range of common coping strategies in their movement toward public leadership.[64] The most common approach used by women speakers from a minority community involves (1) the art of reframing the issue from the speaker's point of view, (2) the strategy of proposing positive action and, finally, (3) accepting the value of the audience's point of view before they have a chance to accept or reject the speaker. Most of Kitano's examples of problem-solving strategies are applicable to speech-development and can be found in speeches by African-American women leaders such as the late Congresswoman Barbara Jordan, Professor Lani Guinier, and Advocate Marion Wright Edelman, all of whom are excellent speakers and role models for all women, not just for women of color. One sociologist explains that Jordan's "choice of words and her dramatic style of speaking made her a national star . . . . it was an inspiring thing to hear—the absolute, clarion, unambiguous sense of moral righteousness."[65]

Myths and Assumptions about Women of Color

If you are a person of color seeking to be seen and heard, the stakes are higher. You are shouldering the history and perceptions of our American experiment. When you stand before a primarily male or white audience, you join other women leaders who are breaking new ground. Women of color may believe that they have left their parents' cultural identity behind, or they may celebrate their heritage and at the same time feel that it has little impact on their public voice. But when a general audience is skeptical about the speaker's credentials, credibility, and ability to connect to the mainstream culture (or the audience's culture), that speaker must plan for the possibility of a biased audience.

Stereotypes are deeply ingrained and remain pervasive in our society, if only found at the level of an individual's subconscious, but they can lead listeners to jump to conclusions about the speaker and where she is coming from, both literally and figuratively. There are stereotypes about everyone in a particular group having certain traits, attitudes, and abilities that can be damaging. When it comes to credibility as a speaker, there is little margin of error for women in our society, and even less for the speaker who is a woman of color. It is likely that what people think about first is that you are a woman and then, that you are "different" based on your race, culture, or ethnicity. If you are Black, Hispanic, Asian, Middle Eastern, or Native American, your presentation style may be judged more critically and by a different set of expectations and conventional standards. Listeners may not even realize how many critical filters they are using that distract them from paying full attention to the message. You must be aware of this possibility when you prepare your remarks so that you can be clear, direct, well-informed, well-organized, and non-defensive. Knowing it is necessary to quickly gain the audience's confidence in your expertise can add additional stress to your anxiety about public speaking.

The irony is that it is hard to grasp the escalating complexity of our interracial, intercultural society. After all, the Black woman facing us might be Indian, or Sephardim. Her married name may only serve to further confuse us if we wish to pigeonhole her. Appearances can be deceiving, and given cultural complexities, population mobility, and intermarriage, we have limited capacity to evaluate a speaker's heritage. Audience members might be surprised by the position that a speaker takes on a particular issue because they inaccurately pegged her.

If you are a woman of color, appearing out of context can place you at risk. Anita Perez Ferguson recalls what happened to Congresswoman Carrie Meek (Florida), who is African American, during her first weeks at the capital in Washington, D.C.:

> *She was excited about her new responsibilities and just a little anxious, so she decided to go to the office on Saturday. Because the Congress was not in session, she had dressed casually and entered the building with the throngs of weekend tourists. As she entered the elevator closest to her office she received some resistance from the operator. 'This elevator is reserved for members only,' the employee, also an African American, stated politely. There ensued a fifteen-minute confrontation during which the security guards were called in to assist until Rep. Meek could prove her status as a duly elected member of the United States Congress.*

If a member of Congress had her authority challenged simply because she was an African-American woman, it is likely that any woman of color in a leadership role will have her authority challenged, whether or not as explicitly as in this telling incident.

Have you ever been given a chance to speak as "the token woman," or as the token woman of color? Political correctness can backfire. For example, when the audience assumes that you were chosen to be on a panel simply because you are a woman of color, neither the audience nor you can do their best thinking. In such a case, eyes are open but ears and minds are closed. The audience may only grudgingly accept your assignment to the panel, and the meat and heart of your presentation can be undervalued in the process. Incorrect assumptions made about your appropriateness as the speaker can be wholly inaccurate but nonetheless damaging to your credibility as a leader and as the voice of authority. These could be assumptions about your limited education, the narrowness of your customs or religious beliefs, a lack of exposure to the arts, or your inability to relate to mainstream middle-class issues. In any case, if you want to address the possibility of your audience's skepticism about your leadership ability or expertise, it is especially important to be well-prepared. This means thoroughly knowing your material and also knowing your audience well enough so that you can find common ground.

Managing Stereotypical Expectations

Audience misperceptions may initially distance the audience from the speaker. There is no simple formula to make an audience feel comfortable with a speaker but it is neither necessary nor desirable for a speaker to change the substance of her character or ignore her background in order to accommodate that dynamic tension. You can deliver a confident and compelling public presentation by being who you are. You can make a statement by your style of dress. You can use folktales that no one has ever heard before. Try the "Asian Folktales" series including *Sohab and Rostum* from Iran, *The Emperor and the Nightingale from China*, or *The Chess Player from Mongolia*.[66] Cultural proverbs carry messages that are universal and timeless. You can use proverbs as strategies to support your proposal or defend your position. Audiences enjoy learning something new or leaving with a quote or proverb to share.

Make your issue matter to everyone. Place your issue within a larger social context so that diverse listeners can relate to it, too. If you want to win an audience over, you must help them by quickly drawing a connection between your topic, product, or proposal and the listeners' needs, concerns, and goals. To do this, you need to overcome the possible perception of insurmountable cultural and/or gender differences that separate you from the diverse, homogeneous, or white male audience. Even if it seems that your audience is as different from you as night from day, you must stretch yourself to find at least one thread of connection. You'll be able to grab their attention and keep it once you can answer these questions:

First, what concerns do we share? *Do we all care about safety in the streets? A reliable pension plan? Quality healthcare? Excellence in Public Service?* Provide solutions to those common concerns, and you'll grab their attention. Second, what do you have in common? Your audience may look very different from you at first glance, but there's always the possibility that you have something in common that is basic to everyone. *Do we not all want the best for our families? How about the pace of life today that is fast and demanding, with not enough personal time? Are we members of the same generation? Did we experience the Vietnam War?* Find that common thread that allows the audience to transcend their first impressions and pay attention to the content of your presentation.

You are unique. Stereotypes are obstacles to making personal contact and establishing good communication between you, as a unique individual, and your audience. Assuming that the audience is operating—even subconsciously—under any inaccurate or outdated misperceptions, you would need to challenge their stereotypical assumptions in those first few minutes by the way in which you are introduced, present yourself, and introduce your material. You must quickly let the audience see you for the unique individual that you are. The memorable speaker is someone who is hard to label. When giving testimony, you would do well to describe your educational background and/or those practical real-world accomplishments that complement, supplement, or compensate for a lack of formal and advanced academic degrees. There is nothing wrong with having earned an advanced degree from 'the school of hard knocks.'

Legislative Aide Priya Dayananda, who described herself as an Indian Christian, hopes to run for Congress someday. She reminds us about the complexity of multicultural societies when she said in an interview that she felt the gap between her views and those, say, of a Punjabi or Hindu Indian American. An audience member could attempt to make assumptions about her background, but she defies stereotypes. Dayananda said, "I will celebrate Diwali, Eid, Jain, and Sikh holidays. That has been my upbringing." If she runs for Congress she says she will do so as "Priya"—a unique individual—and not "Priya, the Indian American."[67]

What strategies will you take to manage the predictable stereotypes that might interfere with your listener's ability to pay attention to your presentation? Given your ethnic, cultural, racial, or religious background, it's important to predict what position the audience expects you to take, and whether you, in fact, do hold this position. *How do you convey that you are not a single-issue spokesperson and that you can see "the big picture?" Have you made it clear that, despite superficial or significant differences, that you have found common ground with your audience?* Given stereotypical expectations, whatever position you take may disappoint or surprise some, many, or all of the listeners.

Challenges Create Champions and Role Models for Every Woman

In spite of the challenges they face in gaining public recognition for the many roles they play, women of color have made enormous contributions to society for many generations, balancing full-time responsibilities for their families with participation in the workforce. Countless religious, educational, cultural, and social organizations have benefited from the dedication and service of women of color.

Women of color do have historical role models who spoke up for justice and democracy for all women. Reading the few examples of brilliant speeches given by women in earlier centuries continues to be inspiring, and many of their ideas remain fresh even today.[68] By observing confident speakers who are women of color, we can learn what delivery styles and strategies work most effectively.

Everyone agrees that Oprah Winfrey, African-American television personality and media executive, is an outstanding communicator. In a commencement speech delivered at Wellesley College, Winfrey inspires others by describing the origins of her life journey:

When I was a little girl [in] Mississippi, growing up on

the farm [with] only Buckwheat as a role model, watching my grandmother boil clothes in a big, iron pot through the screen door, because we didn't have a washing machine and made everything we had, I realized somehow inside myself, in the spirit of myself, that although this was segregated Mississippi and I was "colored" and female, that my life could be bigger, greater than what I saw. I remember being four or five years old, I certainly couldn't articulate it, but it was a feeling, and a feeling that I allowed myself to follow. [69]

Nationally known speakers believe that "authenticity," or being who you are, is a key to delivering effective presentations. If this is true, then women of color may find that being authentic presents a special challenge in the process of connecting with the audience. If appearance and conformity set a standard for early acceptance and identification, then women of color are immediately on the other side of that barrier when they look different from their audience.

How do you overcome the stereotypical biases that can become barriers to making contact with people who are different from you? One way is to construct a gracious introduction that draws upon similar interests with the audience members. A gentle bit of humor will put the audience at ease. For example, a former agricultural worker who overcame the odds and became a businesswoman might bridge a culture gap when addressing chamber of commerce members at their annual dinner:

This is the first time I've ever been to a country club, so I brought along a few of my friends to give me courage. I was thinking of them as we had our meal. My friend Hilda picks the kind of lettuce that we had in our salad. Yolanda packs the strawberries that were in our dessert. And my cousin Dolores in Columbia helps grow the cof-

fee that we are enjoying now. All four of us are as con-
cerned with the quality and safety of the food we pro-
vide for our families, as are all of you. So I'm glad you
invited me to talk with you today about nutrition.

Build a bridge between yourself and your audience. If
you are a woman of color, you must be mindful of drawing
upon your particular cultural heritage in ways that link to
our common humanity. In addition, use your personality to
warm up your audience.

Wilma Mankiller, former chief of the Cherokee Nation,
uses humor to put her audience at ease.

This young man came out to the airport to pick me up
... and he asked me, he said, 'Well, since principal chief
is a male term, how should I address you?' ... I just
looked out the window of the car. Then he said 'Well,
should we address you as chiefteness?' So I looked out
the window for a little longer. Then he thought he
would get real funny and cute, and he asked me if he
should address me as 'chiefette,' so I looked out the win-
dow for a real long time ... and so I told him to call me
'Ms. Chief', (as in) mischief.[70]

Anita Perez Ferguson also likes to make the audience
smile and put them at ease, even when discussing a serious
subject such as diversity. She has often begun her presentations by jokingly correcting the person who introduced her
and giving the audience her full name: "Anita Maria Perez de
Gonzalez Ferguson." For dramatic emphasis, she adds the
slightest pause before saying "... Ferguson." This gives her
the chance to personalize her topic as she proceeds:

What we are really here to talk about is not the abstract
concept of 'diversity' as it relates to affirmative action
programs or fears about quotas, but rather to changes

in our population and workforce brought about by
families in transition—families like those represented
by me and you.

Today, we all know people whose spouse or "significant other" is from a different ethnic, racial, cultural, and/or religious background, or we are one of those people with a hyphenated last name, and her introduction helps us relate to her topic.

Women of color often refer to their mothers and fathers' community-based activism and philanthropic work as a source of inspiration. They relate family anecdotes as a way of emphasizing how their personal journey toward current policy positions developed from their family roots. This is evident in remarks made by The Honorable Alexis Herman, who was the first African American to serve as U.S. Secretary of Labor in the Clinton administration. Her use of self-disclosure links her to everyone in the audience seeking meaningful work.:

> *I was raised by a single mother who rose from an eter-*
> *nity of odd jobs to complete her college education and*
> *fulfill her life's dream of becoming a teacher. My father*
> *beat the odds by becoming a pioneer in business and*
> *politics at a time when there were few opportunities for*
> *African Americans in the South. At home, in school,*
> *and at church, I learned that, after family and faith, the*
> *most sacred thing in our lives is the work we do . . . . For*
> *all of us, our work affirms our humanity, and allows us*
> *to make our own unique contribution to the world.*[71]

Every individual wants to find work that is meaningful, regardless of her or his background, and it is particularly meaningful to hear a Black woman address the subject, given the history of Blacks as slaves in this country.

Even with a culture of modesty, Hispanic women are

178 ∿ *Women Seen and Heard*

breaking new ground. Television producer and journalist Cristina Saralegui speaks about controversial issues in ways that are relevant to her culture. For example, she began a breast cancer awareness project targeting Hispanic women because the Hispanic culture of modesty required a new approach to the subject. She has also addressed gay issues targeting Hispanic teens. In an interview, she said:

> *What I try to do is play down the differences. We're all parents and we have the same problems. I try to appeal to the common denominator . . . everyone is in this together.*[72]

The effective speaker is self-disclosing in a way that engenders respect. You must be unafraid to let the audience see you as a woman who plays many roles in the family and in society, in general: a doctor who is a daughter, a lawyer who is a mother, a health activist who is a sister and a daughter, or a union leader who is raising eleven children. In some ways the woman of color is a unique individual. In some ways she is like women who share her cultural background. In some ways, however, the woman of color is *every woman*, capable of inspiring diverse women and men to follow her lead.

As poet and speaker Maya Angelou reveals:

> *I speak to the Black experience, but I am always talking about the human condition—about what we can endure, dream, fail at, and still survive.*[73]

The more comfortable you are in giving a voice to your own cultural, racial, or ethnic identity and life experience, the more likely it is that you will become both the message and the messenger of hope for the new century.

LESSON
A woman of color must first overcome the audience's preconceptions before she can be seen and heard as a credible leader.

Section Four

SPEAKER SUCCESS

CHAPTER 11

Credibility As the Voice of Authority

Hill alleged that the Supreme Court nominee had repeatedly made sexually offensive comments to her in an apparent campaign of seduction. Hill initially requested that the Senate Judiciary Committee not make public the details of her charges, but the controversy was such that beginning on October 11, 1991, four days of televised hearings were held on the allegations. Americans were shocked by both the frankness of Hill's lurid testimony and the unsympathetic response of the all-male committee, some of whom were openly antagonistic toward Hill. Thomas, meanwhile, denied the charges, and some witnesses called on his behalf cast doubt on Hill's character and mental stability.[74]
—Excerpted from The History Channel

The opposition to taking a woman speaker seriously can be seen when Anita Hill, a law professor at the University of Oklahoma, stepped forward to accuse Supreme Court nominee Clarence Thomas of sexual harassment. She presented her responses to Senators' questions in a quiet manner that was anything but histrionic, and yet her credibility was found suspect. The gender gap was alive and well when it came to evaluating Hill's testimony. Most women believed she was telling the truth. Most men didn't. Ten years later when she delivered a speech at Stanford University reflecting about the hearings, Anita's audience wore buttons claiming, "We believed Anita Hill!"

The Credibility Gap

Audiences may be skeptical about the speaker's credibility because of subconscious stereotypes about women as a group as well as the individual woman's ability to be a leader. In addition, the same stereotypes that can lead an audience to be skeptical about the woman-as-leader may have been internalized by the speaker and cause her to doubt herself, exacerbating her anxiety about public speaking. She may worry, a la Sally Fields speech at the Oscar award ceremony, "Will they like me?" The speaker's anxiety, in turn, may lead her to be less forceful, or self-effacing, to worry too much about what people will think and to soften her main points.

Men, on the other hand, are expected to be opinionated. Scholar Cheris Kramerae writes that ". . . the speech of individual men may be called overbearing or illogical—but as a class, men are not thought to be poor speakers."[75] Women have a different problem; they are not expected to be public speakers, period.

Obviously, then, at the podium men start with credibility. Credibility is men's to lose and women's to win. And yes, a boring speaker is a boring speaker, but women don't have the same luxury as men do in maintaining the audience's attention until the moment they tune out the boring speaker. They need to quickly establish credibility from the get-go and maintain a lively gait. How does a woman establish credibility as a leader through public speaking?

First, becoming an effective speaker involves managing the audience's likely skepticism about your leadership capabilities. It means challenging your own attitudes about the value of your opinions, ideas, and feelings. Second, role models can share the lessons learned by trial and error. Mentors can demonstrate speaking techniques and strategies and coach their protegees. Third, business opportunities, civic involvement, or grass roots activism provide opportunities to participate in discussions and practice giving brief presentations. There are many pathways to success.

Achieving leadership must become women's new work, and in order to become a leader, women must speak effectively in public. Women today want a place at the table—a place where our voices help shape the new century's social and economic agenda. Senator Barbara Boxer believes that:

> *It's time for new priorities. People understand that it's time . . . . Women have got to get involved in the political process, because that's where the power is—the power to make life better for our families and our people.*[76]

When a woman does achieve leadership on boards or in business, government, education, or politics, she will retain that position as much through her skills as a public speaker as through knowledge of her subject matter.

Good speakers have the opportunity to influence the audience's attitudes and behavior, which is a form of power. And leadership is about power—the power to mobilize resources and people. In the past, leaders have gained power through inherited wealth or political clout, personal charisma, networks, and—of course—through intellectual brilliance, personal achievements, and expertise. Audiences remain skeptical about women's capacity for having or gaining the kind of power we associate with male leadership. Audiences expect leaders to look and sound like men. After all, powerful leaders look like Gregory Peck, Lee Iacocca, or Peter Jennings.[77]

As a woman speaker, your initial task is to convince your

audience that you are credible as a leader, that you know what you're talking about, and that you are speaking as "the voice of authority." All speakers need to get their message across to groups and audiences. But unlike men, women also need to overcome audience skepticism about their capacity to be leaders. In order to accomplish these two goals, women speakers must be strategic about using their expertise as a way of gaining credibility, emphasizing the source of their expertise up front, perhaps more so than they might be comfortable doing. They must present ideas in a way that creates confidence in their competence. Otherwise, why would people consider their proposals or requests? Forget the feminine virtues; modesty has no place in this strategy. Women should consider the many areas of life in which they do know what they're talking about and can speak to audiences from experience.

"Women's Ways of Knowing"

Recent research from women psychologists proposes that women have "a different way of knowing"[78] from men, one that is based on their life experiences and the ways in which they have been socialized. Women's expertise is not limited to the conventional and legitimate sources of knowledge such as education, training, and occupational experience or published research; rather, it also includes knowledge gained from creatively coping with the stressors of juggling diverse and often contradictory roles. In addition to life experience, your expertise also comes from what you've learned from many other sources besides conventional activies. These include your grass-roots activism, community involvement, from reading voraciously about your favorite subject, your travels abroad, being on a nonprofit board, and your ability to use technology. When you speak to groups, you certainly need not be apologetic if your wisdom comes from in-depth life experience rather than from academic or professional knowledge; rather, you can emphasize the wide variety of experiences that have created your base of knowledge.

Women's roles require them to take charge of family life: they must purchase and prepare foods, balance the family budget, care for children, and attend to aging parents, just a few tasks that involve skills and competencies gained outside of academics. Our society may not give you the credit due for your responsibilities in this domain, but you should. Women provide continuity in an otherwise fragmented world. Being a daughter, sister, wife, or mother means that you have probably learned and maintained certain historic cultural rituals commemorating transitions such as marriage, menses, manhood, birth, healing practices, holidays, widowhood, and death. How can you relate your knowledge of these rituals to your topic? What audiences would find your knowledge of these rituals particularly interesting? Women rarely think strategically about the value of what they know from playing conventional roles, but they could, and it might be fascinating to those outside that experience.

Fewer women are in the role of fulltime wife and mother as a result of later marriages, involvement in fulltime careers, and widowhood. Because of this shift, more women are going to challenge conventional perceptions of family life. Add differences in women's background, cultural and racial differences, and the gender equation becomes more complex. As a speaker, you need to figure out whether your audience would find this gender difference valuable. For example, given your background, how would you address these questions:

1. How would you define the term "family values"?
2. How can older women save adequately for retirement?

3. How might you design housing for today's single career woman or working parents?

We each could discuss such topics based on our unique way of understanding these issues, and also, on how we've played out our assigned cultural, racial, and gender roles.

Women are beginning to gain political power with help from the vast storehouse of experiential knowledge, friendships, and networks that they have accumulated over the years from managing households and being involved in their schools, communities, and churches. The ever-widening gender gap in American politics attests to this gain in political power. In fact, in recent elections, women determined who was elected governor and senator.[79] Women's life experiences will make an impact on our society in many ways, to include such topics as:

☐ how women are changing the professions of law, medicine, and architecture

☐ research on women's health issues that no longer considers the male body to be the basis for clinical trials

☐ community development and redevelopment projects that consider the needs of women, children, and families

☐ workplace practices and legislation that consider women's multiple roles

☐ social and economic policy debates that include women at the table.

Simply because you're a woman, your perspective is different from a man's and, as such, your life experiences provide you with a different and often undervalued base of knowledge. You can flaunt those differences in gaining credibility as the voice of authority.

Grass-Roots Activism

Are you a grass-roots activist? If so, you've learned by doing, not from an academic course. A grass-roots activist becomes a catalyst for change when she shares new information with neighbors, friends, or coworkers. The news may be good or bad. It may be local; for example, a company is going-out-of-business, a school is changing vacation policies, a county dump is being proposed near your company, or a tragic accident creates urgency around the need for a traffic signal at a busy intersection. The news may be global: for example, a new airport security measure is worth sharing with others. Talking about what's current, what's changing, or what's needed is the first step in becoming a grass-roots activist. Have you ever taken that step? If you did, could you share the lessons learned with an audience?

Second, we've all known people most affected by a situation who band together to solve a common problem, perhaps by proposing a new policy or getting a voter initiative on the ballot that creates new legislation. Grass-roots activism is distinctly different from the policy-driven change resulting from staff research by those who work for the government, academia, or a corporation. Actor/producer Rob Reiner became an activist for preschool children, and to the dismay of politicians, his successful California initiative produced enormous tobacco tax revenues to better coordinate existing programs and fund new educational programs for young children; the funding may well dignify and professionalize the role of child-care workers. Malcolm Gladwell, whose book *Tipping Point*[80] is a study of how change occurs in modern settings, calls people like Reiner who see a need and initiate social change "connectors" or "mavens." Similarly, women have naturally been good connectors through informal networking in their private lives; this same skill can be politicized in public presentations when a speaker connects the dots for her audience.

Are you old enough to remember Betty Friedan's book, *The Feminine Mystique*?[81] Perhaps your mother will, or perhaps you had to read it for a sociology class. The book transcended the author's expectations when she wrote it in 1964, creating an unlikely generation of grass-roots activists. Women began to meet in small discussion groups to address the issues it raised, and soon began to collectively take action, forming grass-roots organizations in neighborhoods and a national organization that ultimately pressured legislators for more equitable employment practices and civil rights legislation. Even the most unlikely bedfellows (or sisters) can become grass-roots activists over a local issue of common concern.

Developing expertise through grass-roots activism doesn't happen overnight. Activists begin by seeking out others who share their concerns, spending time framing issues and planning strategic activities. Initially, they organize themselves as groups of interested volunteers and, at some point, realize they must give testimony, or address the school board, city council, board of supervisors, or state legislature. This requires finding a spokesperson who can speak with passionate conviction about their common cause. Trying to block a pending policy or gain endorsement of a new policy is different from preaching to the choir. Forming coalitions with other groups and governmental agencies becomes critical in order to mobilize support and get the word out. If you are going to succeed as a leader, you must learn new skills, including the art of persuasion and debate.

Grass-roots leaders tenaciously work toward a satisfactory resolution of a common problem by ensuring that their group gets a fair hearing and that there is follow-through on their proposal. When an activist becomes a leader it is because she has figured out how to direct the group's concerns to the right decision-makers with authority and resources. Although the beginning steps of sharing information are often natural and comfortable for many people, the leader stands out because she stays focused, continually communicating with the group and other stakeholders, and remaining visible through public speaking activities.

The same skills that allowed you to achieve success in your grass-roots activist role can lead you to other leadership roles. For example, Doreen Farr was a homemaker preparing to become a teacher. One day she heard bulldozers on the property next to her home and became concerned. After her individual efforts at trying to modify this project failed, she began to interact with other homeowners who had similar concerns about what they perceived as rampant development in their neighborhood. By offering her support to others who were organizing regional planning efforts, Farr became a spokesperson for her area. Soon an elected official invited her to become a planning commissioner, and from there she rose to the position of chairperson. When Farr speaks to others today, she makes it apparent that her planning expertise began with trying to resolve her own problem.

A grass-roots activist from Vermont, Jody Williams reached the pinnacle of public attention when she won the 1996 Nobel Peace Prize, only the twenty-ninth woman to do so in its one hundred year history. Jody previously worked in Central America, where she had observed the devastating effect of land mines on civilians, even after military actions had ceased in this region. Organizing individuals and groups, Jody began a movement that culminated in an international treaty that banned the use of land mines. Her expertise and tenacity was put to the test as she developed a successful grass-roots campaign through her speeches and presentations.

When they speak to a group or audience, grass roots activists can have credibility for two reasons. First, they have gained in-depth knowledge about an issue and can speak with great specificity about the history of a problem, as well as the facts, figures, policies, and legal actions taken. Second, they can inspire and guide other individuals and groups to organize a grass-roots campaign around their particular local issue. However, activists must speak to a group or audience in a way that convinces listeners that they are the voice of authority, or they won't be effective.

Expertise Gained from Experience

If you work in a field in which the flow of information or access to current and accurate information is never-ending, you're at an advantage. By contrast, a community activist or nonprofit board member can't substantiate current knowledge as easily as can someone who is immersed in research in her field and enjoys peer and staff support. However, you do have talented people available to help you. Staff members who work for or with your elected and appointed state and federal officials will help constituents with necessary research. They are able to easily find the most accurate and current demographic information and census data, and provide you with policy and legislative updates. Their assistance is invaluable to any speaker who wants to further develop her expertise on a particular topic.

There are other ways to find assistance in gaining access to current information and new ideas. College student interns are available to help you track down information and conduct interviews. Doctoral students in the arts, humanities, technology, and the social and hard sciences at a local university are always conducting research to test hypotheses about problems; these students can be found with help from the university staff of a particular department. Medical and law school librarians are a wonderful source of assistance when you're seeking factual information. Many websites exist for easy access to information relevant to women's issues and concerns, or general topics researched from a woman's point of view. Once you know your target audience's mission and strategic goals, you can seek out accurate and current new information that will be useful to them. In turn, audiences who appreciate your efforts to provide cutting edge information will soon be quoting you.

Once you've finished your research, what do you do with all this information? First of all, don't overwhelm audiences. Your time at the podium is limited, so sift through the data and find those interesting contradictions or significant omissions. Raise questions that the conventional wisdom has missed, and track down the answers. Wake up your audience with current information. For example:

◆ *Here are the shocking mortality statistics for women of our age group.*

◆ *Here are the surprising statistics on federally employed women's income post retirement.*

◆ *Here are amazing comparisons between the success rate of businesses owned by women and men.*

◆ *Here are stunning figures on how skills in budget and finance improve women's earning power.*

A grass-roots activist is an advocate, a free agent who can challenge authority. You have fewer constraints than elected officials who have diverse constituent groups to please. In order to have credibility, however, you'll need to know what you're talking about, having the most current facts available to support your real-world experience.

Expertise from Your Travels

You may not be a CEO or a senator, but your travel experiences can make you the voice of authority. Women who travel the globe—and more are doing so today—have different stories to tell than men do. This doesn't mean a recitation of activities along the lines of "how I spent my summer vacation." In some countries and cultures, women who travel alone are at particular risk. Travel forces you to learn new ways of being resourceful and levelheaded. Audiences will be interested in hearing about what is exotic or how the U.S. compares to other places. Whether you're interested in children, business, or politics, you might address any of these questions for an interesting talk:

- ☐ *How is family life—and the roles of women and men— different in Asia? The Middle East?*

- ☐ *What can we learn from countries in which roles are reversed—where doctors are women and teachers are men?*

- ☐ *How do Western European employers maintain high employee morale?*

- ☐ *How do Scandinavian childcare programs compare to ours?*

- ☐ *What are three common spiritual practices found in Asia that anyone in the U.S. can easily learn and use daily?*

- ☐ *How has the Internet transformed life in the biggest cities in China?*

- ☐ *What are three strategies for feeling safe while traveling alone?*

- ☐ *How can the over-fifty-five traveler on a budget make the rupee, yen, and franc stretch farther?*

Could you address any of these examples? What travel experiences of yours would be interesting to discuss with a small group of friends, coworkers, or a business group in your town? Do you have slides of your trip, art objects, or exotic food to share with your audience? What three lessons have you learned from your travels?

Knowledge or insights gained from travel can substantiate your position as a credible authority. Sharing what you learned can save the listeners time, money, grief, or educate them about a country and culture they may never experience directly. A wonderful slide show or videotape can substantiate your travel experience and show you as an independent woman who can be strategic, plan ahead, and achieve her goals. There you are, traveling on the Yangtze River, riding a camel in a scorching desert, or wearing a burkha while working for the International Red Cross! What better way to instantly convey your credibility as an independent woman than to help the audience place you in that foreign setting? Entertain while you inspire or educate people and you'll be worth your speaker's fee.

Education and Work Experience

If you want the audience to take you seriously then you have to take yourself seriously. Be aware of any tendencies that you have to downplay your education and your abilities. Which kind of expertise best describes you? Check those that apply:

- ☐ I have gained valuable experience by working in a particular occupation or field.
- ☐ I have kept current in my field through readings, continuing education programs, and attendance at conferences.

☐ I have maintained a professional practice (for example, as an educator, lawyer, doctor, or engineer.

☐ I have conducted scientific research.

☐ I have passed licensing exams.

☐ I have produced published documents.

☐ I have spoken at conferences.

Any one of the above descriptions indicates that you have achieved a certain standard of performance and that you have the potential to speak knowledgeably about your subject based on your training and accomplishments. You have information that your audience needs to know.

While women's modesty is required in certain cultures, even liberated American women are not encouraged to brag about their ability to think critically or about their accomplishments as individuals. For example, women typically thank others for their success or attribute their accomplishments to luck rather than to ability. Can you imagine Hillary Clinton saying "Everything I am I owe to my husband?" That may have been common years ago, but today's active women have gained skills and knowledge the old fashioned way: cultivating their abilities, working hard, gaining training and an education, and displaying loyalty to their profession. The audience needs to understand that your success was at least partially the result of the cultivation of your abilities. If your presentation is well organized, on point, and related to the audience, your performance as a speaker will reflect those skills and abilities.

Publications

You can always write about your expertise or use writing as a way of developing your expertise. Many opportunities exist to be published, and published authors are desirable speakers. Web companies seek articles. Business magazines such as *Fast Company* are open to hearing new ideas that represent women and ethnic/cultural diversity in the high-tech fields. Organizational newsletters solicit articles. Just as an example, Lois Phillips' article on how women overextend themselves titled, "Fragmentia: The disease of women in transition,"[82] was later reworked into an article called "Organizational Fragmentia"[83] about organizations that grow too quickly in too many directions at the same time. Each of these publications led to speaking engagements, one for a human resources association and another for a medical school.

The news services may be appropriate places to send brief articles or seek opportunities for syndication. Editors who select Op Ed pieces for the local or regional papers do publish thoughtful pieces about controversial issues, human-interest stories, and current events. Express your opinion, and develop your reasoning in written articles.

Being published is one way of building a sphere of influence. The editor's endorsement of your ideas gives you credibility as an expert, and establishing credibility—both getting it and keeping it—is a key challenge for women leaders. It helps when the person who hires you to speak at the convention can say, "She's been published in numerous magazines or newspapers." Those publications must be referenced in your bio and in the way you're introduced.

Unlike private, informal conversations, which are not documented and poorly remembered, publications become your paper trail and will document when, where, and how you've taken a stand. If you decide to change your mind or position on what you published, you'll need to defend your opinions vigorously and over a significant period of time. Don't fall prey to the stereotype about a woman's inability to make up her mind. A shift in your thinking can be defended as a good thing. Explain to your audience why you've changed your opinion. The world changes, the facts change, and you revised your original position accordingly, as Arianna Huffington did, with great success. In fact, these changes may lead you to write a new Op Ed piece or book.

Anita Perez Ferguson had great success self-publishing her book, *A Passion for Politics: Encouraging Women in Leadership.* Working closely with a copyeditor and consultant, she organized her press clippings, essays, and personal diary describing her two congressional campaigns and leadership at the National Women's Political Caucus. The book's development and publication process were creative capstones, helping Anita to give the campaigns renewed meaning and reach closure on her experience. A business consultant advised her to distribute the book to some conference audiences free of charge as part of her fee. Status as an author greatly helped her to negotiate contracts with statewide and national audiences, and she quickly recouped the price of publishing the book through these contracts. Do you have a book inside you?[84]

Board Membership

Many women are active on volunteer boards but don't adequately appreciate the value of their involvement. Volunteers are the engines of American society and its social service agencies and commissions. The meaning of your membership on a nonprofit board of directors goes beyond the philanthropic. It's also educational, a great way to learn firsthand about social issues in your community or across the nation. Often board members are attracted to an agency because of the work that it does. They imagine that they can work behind the scenes to help staff and management achieve their goals, but they don't realize that part of the director's role is to deliver public presentations. Board members may be willing to be generous with their own funds, write letters, attend events, and cajole friends to jump on the bandwagon, but how enthused are they when it comes to speaking to the city council, boards, foundations, or potential donors? Are they comfortable raising money and persuading donors, charities, or foundations that *their* organization is more worthy than other agencies? Inevitably, effective board members have to convince someone: *My nonprofit agency is worth your money, and let me tell you why.*

Let's face it: it's easier to fight for someone in need than for your personal advancement. Being on a board is a great way to develop and polish your presentation skills because of the "P.Q."—your passion quotient. The more you immerse yourself in an agency's work through board membership, the more anecdotes you'll collect to share with audiences. Combine anecdotes with hard hitting facts while conveying your passion for your nonprofit agency, and you'll be more credible at the podium.

It's fun to schmooze up interesting people at fundraisers, but ultimately the successful board member is someone whose presentations have a positive and tangible outcome, such as receiving funding from a grant or a large contribution from a new donor, positive press coverage, or a new facility. Those articulate board members who have conquered their fears of public speaking will be the heavy hitters on a local board. Often, these are the people who are tapped for statewide and national leadership roles.

Board membership is also an excellent way to cultivate expertise about broader social issues that go beyond the particular work of an agency. You can take your knowledge to the larger community, educating people who make decisions about resources, programs, and community needs. You can share your ideas in public forums, give testimony, or be a panelist in an educational program.

The good news is that speaking to the public gets easier as you go. Each prepared set of slides, handouts, quotes, and statistics can be the building block for the next presentation. You won't have to reinvent the wheel once you have built the factual and technical foundation. Having these materials handy means it takes less time to prepare for subsequent presentations, then you can focus on the specific needs of subsequent audiences and build a collection of relevant anecdotes, cartoons, shocking statistics, and dramatic or poignant headlines. You can extend your collection of materials by sharing them with other board members who are becoming skilled presenters.

Research Skills

An expert is someone who understands current trends in her subject area. These may include social, economic, and industrial trends that reflect the latest demographic and census-based research. Stay current with discoveries occurring every day in technology industries as they apply to your field of interest. Speakers need to stay ahead of the curve; you'll want to be one step ahead of the audience on your subject.

Social commentaries indicate that people are on information overload. The Internet provides access to a global database, but sorting through it all is impossible for the lay person. Audiences appreciate knowing that the information you present is current and accurate, and, perhaps even more important, that it will help them achieve their goals.

How do you focus on the right information for your audiences? We're probably all reading similar mainstream newspapers and magazines, so why not read the alternative press as excerpted in the *Utne Reader?* Professional or technical journals will provide you with the latest information—the same information that practitioners require. Remember that the general lay public isn't reading the same material as doctors, lawyers, engineers, and other specialists. If you want to keep up to date, you can access current research online or at your local university library.

When speaking to business and professional audiences in particular, you need to demonstrate that you are informed with hard data and current research that relates to your point of view in the context of broader social, political, or business concerns. Executive digest newsletters, which summarize current thinking by popular management gurus, make it easier to track trends in the business world. If you want to be able to use common references to fiction chosen by the public at large, listen to a bestseller on tape or read book reviews. The top universities publish management journals and provide audiotapes and videotapes of conference proceedings for those who are interested in hearing from the academic community. Your ability to use the language, concepts, and terminology crafted by other leaders puts you in good company and adds to your credibility.

Technical Expertise

If you don't overdo it, PowerPoint software can be useful in conveying the key points of a complex presentation to an audience unfamiliar with your data. Make a statement about how comfortable you are with technology, thereby negating stereotypes about how all women lack technical sophistication. The presentation software is useful in forcing you to organize ideas logically and systematically. Scan in photos, graphs, and charts to visualize your key points. We always caution clients to have only a few bullet points or one visual per slide in order to keep the audience focused on you, the speaker. If you're not proficient in this technology, local graphic design firms or copy shops can produce the materials you need. Other technologies can also assist you in delivering polished and organized presentations; for example, large electronic whiteboards can be used to record and print discussion notes. A laptop computer can be connected to the World Wide Web to demonstrate a point.

How many times have you seen a speaker disappear into the darkness as she or he proceeds to narrate their slide show? Professional speakers know that they need to be well lit when they're on stage. Even when showing slides or a brief excerpt of a film, the speaker needs to remain visible. A darkened room puts people to sleep. The audience is paying to see and hear *you*, not the technology, which is merely a tool to illustrate your point. Overheads are fine for pro bono presentations but paid presentations require more sophisticated visual aids.

Visuals can be utilized to provide visual evidence of the speaker's mastery of her topic. Former Astronaut France Cordova, now Chancellor at the University of California at Riverside, has utilized pictures of space taken from one of her research projects. The woman who climbed Mount Everest produced a slide show, providing her view from the top. Marie Wilson of the Ms. Foundation shows a video of the girls who receive financial support for their projects, giving her organization a human face. If you're not a technical person, crack an egg, count jelly beans in a jar, or demonstrate how to stand on your head. Whatever you do, use visuals and/or your physical presence to keep your talk lively.

The medium is the message. When you speak in a public voice, you are the center of attention for at least a few moments. Do you have a commanding presence? Will you take charge of the space around the podium and be a lively presenter, or will you stand rigidly with your hands in a prayer position? How you move about and take up space is a metaphor for your ability to be a leader, and to be actively involved. Does your image convey confidence in your expertise?

Even Before You Speak, Your Introduction Speaks for You

Your CQ—credibility quotient—as an authority begins with the introduction. Too often, the program moderator's introduction consists of reading lengthy lists from the speaker's resume, which can put the audience to sleep. Sometimes the praise is well intentioned and effusive but nonspecific, such as "You're going to love her! She's great!" This is very different from "Angelina Broder can interpret demographic information for us in ways that will help us market our new service." Thus, when planned in advance, the introduction can set the stage for the audience's readiness to take you seriously as a leader.

Each speaking situation is unique. Perhaps you want to emphasize your personal travels and de-emphasize your technical and occupational skills and experience. Why leave anything to chance? Write the brief introduction yourself and hand it to the person who will introduce you. Make sure the text of the introduction selectively highlights those aspects of your background that would be relevant to the audience and to the occasion.

For a more compelling presentation, balance professional and occupational knowledge with the personal knowledge you've gained from observations of practical everyday life. Audiences will love to hear a speaker challenge a conventional perspective:

> *'They say' has been proven a great liar; I've observed quite the opposite perspective from the earlier speech by being an emergency room nurse. Today, I'm going to share several revelations about our inner city patients that will surprise you.*

People love to hear about trade secrets and good gossip in what feels like a conspiratorial exchange.

Audiences are evaluating every aspect of your presentation. You must pull out every stop, use everything you have learned from and experienced in life to engender confidence in your expertise as a credible leader.

LESSON
A woman speaker has many ways to establish credibility as an expert and leader based on life experience and a "woman's way of knowing."

CHAPTER 12

A Speaking Career

You will know whether or not you are benefiting from the lessons learned if you are now speaking to audiences on a regular basis. The feedback you receive is now unsolicited and consistently positive. More requests come your way, and speaking to groups takes up more and more of your time. People are volunteering you to represent your team, group, or association. You've been asked to appear on panels. The press has asked you to comment on current events, controversial issues, or business matters. People are quoting you. Most important, not only are you comfortable speaking to groups, you actually enjoy facing an audience and taking the opportunity to make a difference in how people think and behave. It's now time to consider becoming a paid professional public speaker. A skilled presenter can be paid anywhere from hundreds to thousands of dollars to inform, inspire, motivate, or persuade her audience.

What Am I Worth?

Why will groups pay you to speak? First, conferences and special programs have budgets and expect to pay speakers who can help them get a turnout for their event, and who will motivate and meet the needs of their audience. Second, you have already invested the equivalent of months or years becoming versed in your subject matter and, as the expression goes, "time is money." Your knowledge saves the listeners money as you bring research summaries and critical thinking to bear when you analyze the pros and cons of a debatable issue. The time you spend preparing your outline, PowerPoint presentation, and handouts, as well as gaining up-to-date information is a drop in the bucket compared to what you already bring to the task. The speaker's presentation is her "product."

As a woman, your fresh voice brings new insights and ways to articulate the problem that is being presented. Social and business problems can be analyzed differently if the subject is viewed with a different lens. These include the need for affordable childcare and affordable housing, the graying of America, eliminating violent crime, improving education, providing good customer service, and meeting the complex needs of new global markets. Women have new ideas about all of these issues and opportunities, and their ideas for products and services can be profitable, whether in helping people make money, save money, or not waste time.

Should you quit your day job? Before doing so, you'll need to seriously evaluate your constitutional predisposition for stress; i.e., the energy required to catapult yourself forward on the initial trajectory, and your financial and psychological ability to cope with the inevitable slow times when the phone doesn't ring.

If you choose to become a full-time public speaker as your primary source of income, you'll have to overcome the limitations of your own modesty, a trait that is common to many women who have been raised to be polite, humble, and self-effacing. If this is true of you, marketing yourself as a paid professional speaker may be uncomfortable. After all, society expects women to volunteer their time to community groups, and groups will often ask you to volunteer to be their speaker for a monthly meeting or special program on a pro bono basis. You may be tempted to volunteer to speak about your favorite topic on a pro bono basis, particularly if you feel a passionate conviction about the issue. Perhaps the adrenaline rush you receive from speaking is reward enough. Although it's easy to volunteer, you need to resist temptation because you've already completed your learning curve and are now a skilled presenter with expertise to share. There is no reason why you should not seek payment for a presentation.

Fee schedules for speakers vary, and the best way to find your scale is to talk to other speakers or organizations that pay speakers. Becoming a freelance professional speaker is easier for political, literary, or film icons. It's not uncommon to be paid $1,500 or $2,500 for a lunchtime presentation as the keynote speaker, or up to $50,000 if you're a former secretary of state or popular governor. Most of us don't qualify for large fees unless our accomplishments or our point of view are indeed unique. If you decide to be a freelance speaker, you'll need to increase your visibility as an articulate individual by developing marketing materials, and contracting with the right audiences that want to hear your perspective.

Develop fees that are appropriate to your level as well as what the market will bear. Anita and Lois began with $250 fees and slowly graduated upwards. National conference programs will often pay anywhere from $2,500 to $5,000. If you've written a book, you may barter around your fee to be able to sell your book at the conference, which might be more lucrative in the end. If a hundred people purchased a $20 book, that's $2,000. Conference organizers might guarantee you a certain amount of book sales as your fee. There are many ways to negotiate your fees, and a good business coach can assist you in developing a contract.

There is limited value in signing up with a speaker's

bureau. Unless you've written a bestseller and are requesting fees in the $10,000 range, you won't get much attention from an agent. Agents will take about 25 percent of your fee and are most excited about working with celebrities, politicians, or established authors. Most of us must go it alone.

The Role of Paid Spokesperson

It might at first seem hard to believe, but you don't have to quit your day job to *become* a paid speaker. If you enjoy delivering presentations and have developed speaking skills of professional caliber, you can always work inside an organization as their official spokesperson. This is a legitimate form of work. According to legal history, "spokespersons" were predecessors of attorneys as far as back as the eighth century in Europe. Spokespersons had faultless behavior, were honest and familiar with the legal customs of their governments.[85] Today, the Web lists twenty-two thousand references to "spokespersons." They are paid lobbyists, activists, and advocates who can address diverse audiences, including the press, regarding the mission, goals, and activities of their professional associations, nonprofit agencies, corporations, or special interest groups. Being a spokesperson is one way to capitalize on your speaking skills while receiving the benefits and perks of full-time employment.

How do you get hired as a professional spokesperson? Those days of volunteering to give an organizational report can pay off. Representing your team at a managers' meeting can become part of your job description, incorporated into your annual performance review and listed on your resume. Once you've demonstrated presentation skills, you may be tapped as the right person to deliver reports at agency or corporate meetings. Bingo! With each presentation, your visibility increases. You'll be seen as a potential spokesperson for the whole organization once managers realize that you are articulate and can think on your feet.

Also, promoting an insider is efficient. Insiders understand the history and products or services better than a newcomer can. Insiders have the potential to more effectively respond to impromptu questions about the entire organization when speaking to the press, customers, governmental agencies, and other stakeholders.

Speaking to the press involves print and televised interviews. Don't forget that reporters can be confrontational. Your ability to handle the Q and A with reporters will be worth a great deal to your organization. Think about those times spokespersons have been most successful in explaining the nature of crises such as the delayed Red Cross payment to families of the World Trade Center tragedy, poison found in Tylenol capsules, a transportation strike that shuts down a city, or an airplane crash with high fatalities.

As a result of their crisis communication skills, spokespersons can help their organizations avoid costly litigation. The people who handle crisis situations best are well-informed, authentic in their demeanor, straightforward, and sincere. The only downside to being the spokesperson is getting pigeonholed as "the bad news bear." There may be times when the top executive—not the spokesperson—simply has to face the music.

Find Your Niche

Speaker Barbara Mintzer has found her niche in the health-care field. In order to be appropriate for each audience, she customizes her preparation by interviewing several people from the sponsoring organization who will be in her audience to find out the issues that healthcare professionals are facing. She weaves their input into her remarks. From interviews, she soon realized the extent of the stress that healthcare personnel face every day as they work in a rapidly changing environment. As a result, she has become an expert on the topic of "creating opportunities out of today's changes in healthcare." Even though she herself was not in the medical field, her core values as a people-person, experience as a Career Track presenter, and ongoing field research make her a sought-after motivational speaker.

To be successful in finding your niche, you'll need to stay abreast regarding what your audiences need to know. You'll want to do your homework to feel confident that you are in-the-loop; for example:

◆ *What are the hot topics or current events that concern members of the audience?*

◆ *What changes in demographics or the economy are threatening their future?*

Business groups, such as the American Business Women's Association, Soroptimists, Zonta, The Rotary Club, and Society of Women Accountants—to mention a few—are always looking for lively and knowledgeable presenters who can inspire or motivate those who attend their conference meetings. Business groups of men and women continuously seek good speakers. Depending on the planning cycles, professional meeting planners can tell you when and which organizations are on the lookout for speakers. In the non-profit world, boards tend to change in January, which is when the committees start to plan their annual calendar of events.

The key to a professional speaker's success is to find out what the audience needs to know and to decide if there's a fit with what you know. Humor, anecdotes, passionate conviction—all that is part of your charisma—but audiences today are driven by their need for information. If you can make complex information accessible to your audience, you'll find that you're in demand. Lois Phillips did that when she translated complex material from Peter Senge's book, *The Fifth Discipline*, into a workshop format for the nonprofit and educational sector.[86] Her purpose was to train managers in how to build learning organizations, but she had to deliver the key points in a presentation first.

Is your issue the same as everyone else's? Maybe so, but perhaps yours is a unique perspective. Perhaps you have a different style of presenting basic technical information. Can you dramatize the issue as seen in a fictional conversation between two historical figures? Do you have cartoons that can make the audience find humor in a bleak situation? Could you produce a slide show that can inspire us to imagine adapting different forms of housing to your locale, using examples from different countries?

Print and electronic media thrive on conflict and controversy and the next new thing. If you have an alternate point of view about a new social or economic problem that has plagued society for many years, organizations will seek you out. However, don't adopt a point of view after you see which way the wind is blowing just to get the paying gig. Believe in what you're saying or you'll ultimately contradict yourself down the line.

Some speakers challenge the prevailing point of view with outrageous humor. Anita Perez Ferguson heard a speaker ask, "What's wrong with being slightly overweight in a youth-obsessed society?" Her title was "Why a Little Fat May Make You Fit." In the same vein, humorist Margaret Cho pokes fun at Asian culture when she talks about being the overweight sister in her family and dealing with the stereotypes based on "the China doll" syndrome. Cho remarked that "A lot of Asian women told me that they felt grateful that the silence was broken for them."[87] The underlying more serious theme of her presentations actually concerns the power of stereotypes to undercut self-esteem, but women and men can all relate to the human issues of family dynamics.

If you have a fresh take on an old topic that you want to promote through public speaking, your initial job is to locate the audience that is interested in hearing your perspective. You can do this best by talking with people you know who share your interests, asking them for leads about conferences and meetings. Meeting planners are always looking for speakers. The library has reference materials listing all professional associations and organizations by topic.

Marketing Yourself As a Professional Speaker

First, you need to find *your* audience. After you identify the market you're interested in, ask yourself, what market niche exists? What is the conventional wisdom with regard to your topic? Then figure out how your point of view is different from other speakers'. For example, are you physically challenged, a Latina businesswoman, a finance wizard, or the first woman to be hired in your technical position?

Do your homework. Why not interview members or leaders of professions, associations, and groups that can benefit from your ideas? You'll find out more about their current and unmet needs. Speakers aren't paid to express what is already known or believed as "conventional wisdom." Can you provide an alternative to conventional thinking and provoke people to make changes in their lives that are helpful to them? Are there new audiences for the same old topics, or new topics for the usual suspects?

Picking up the phone is never easy. Speaker Barbara Mintzer admits,

> *I have to constantly work on my aversion to marketing myself. The men in my professional support network have no difficulty doing this but [they] are always reminding me to 'toot my own horn more' when I'm marketing my services.*[88]

The first step is to review your list of current contacts. What organizations do they belong to? If any of your contacts are board or program committee members, so much the better because they know how you might fit into an upcoming program. The contacts can suggest to their group that they design an event around your expertise. Has anyone on your contact list seen you speak at a meeting? It's easier to pick up the phone to call someone you know if they've seen you speak. Which people on your list can vouch for the fact that you have expertise and are articulate and a poised presenter? Are you on a listserve? If so, then you have access to a large group of contacts through common interests.

Make an A, B, and C list based on the likelihood of each contact referring you as a speaker. Then, pick up the phone or get on e-mail to market yourself. Start by indicating your interest in speaking to their group and then inquire about upcoming conferences and programs, resources for speakers, contact persons, and deadlines.

Which groups have statewide or national conferences? The local library has catalogues of hundreds of interest-based, service-based, and professional and occupational associations. From acupuncturists to zoologists, there are bound to be many groups of people that would benefit from your expertise. From the basic presentation and the modules you've created, you can easily reorganize your presentation to meet the needs of a particular group. The Internet is probably the best way to update your anecdotes, headlines, research data, and cartoons, allowing you to customize your basic presentation for each new audience. Market your expertise as the voice of authority and recycle your topic in different ways.

The Directory of National Trade and Professional Associations of the United States is an outstanding resource. Published by Columbia Books for about $150, this guide (or the local and regional directory) is a great first investment. It may become your best resource. The number of groups and associations who are potential audiences will surprise you.

Market Your Unique Point of View

If you are a practitioner, you will be able to provide anecdotes and stories that will give people a personal sense of the issue, given your expertise and your competence. There's nothing worse than listening to someone summarize the key points of a bestseller as if he or she were speaking to a third grade class. We can buy the audiotape, thank you very much. But how about a woman discussing such "masculine" topics as the new high-tech global economy, military defense spending, or the uses of robotics in surgery and manufacturing? That's guaranteed to be news to a wide range of groups.

You needn't limit yourself to women's issues such as children, family, education, or healthcare, because women are breaking new ground in formerly all-male professions such as science, medicine, law, architecture, and theology, in addition to technical occupations such as construction, transportation, urban planning, and politics. It's likely that you'll have new ideas about how to relate differently to clients, customers, parishioners, and patients as well as the public at large. Yours is a fresh voice that people will pay attention to. The evaluations of your performance will tell you if your audience enjoyed what they heard and provide suggestions for improvement. If you have succeeded, don't be surprised when audience members ask you to speak to other groups.

The difference in your life experiences and point of view as a woman can help you market a talk about business or social problems. You can identify the need for public health programs from a woman's point of view, as former Assistant Surgeon General Antonia Novella did. You can model a different leadership style as Avon's CEO Andrea Jung did when she supported the idea of corporate involvement in the Breast Cancer Walkathon; this turned out to be a good business decision as well as a demonstration of social responsibility.

Word of Mouth Is the Best Referral

How can you find out which local and statewide groups and associations want speakers for their conference programs? Friends and colleagues in your networks can help you find the contact person.

Word of mouth is the best way to market your services. Once you've been well received by one group you can use this contact to find others. When the contact person says, "Thanks! You did a great job," practice asking, "Do you know any other groups who might enjoy or appreciate this presentation?" Seize those moments when you have a satisfied customer in front of you (or on the phone) to get new leads. It's probably easier for you to have passionate conviction about your message than it is for you to have passionate conviction about your speaking skills, but without continuing to widen your networks and expanding to include new audiences, you'll likely spend your time preaching to the choir (and pro bono, too).

Second, gain endorsements from groups, associations, or institutions based on their satisfaction with your performance. They can attest to the fact that you have something to say and that you will deliver your message in a way that is compelling and memorable. They have found you to be a resource to others. Their endorsement limits the risk to potential clients of hiring an unknown.

Soliciting letters from customers immediately after the event will help. If they don't provide a letter, ask for one that includes your topic and the audience response. Don't be surprised if your customers ask you to craft one for them. Send the first draft off in an e-mail that includes all the logistical information about date, location, conference or program title, audience response, size, and demographics. Usually the customer will add superlatives. Later, once you've compiled a few testimonials, you can prepare a one-page flyer that summarizes a few key phrases from each reference letter along with your photo and contact information at the top.

Use the Media

Develop a press kit with salient information—whatever will help you make your case as a desirable speaker. Anita includes a one-page resume and a scan-able photo, articles or excerpts of articles she's written, or articles about one of her presentations that was newsworthy. Quotes from satisfied meeting planners or clients can more concretely speak to your skills and abilities than you can. Quotes are valuable because they place you in a social, professional, or political context that possibly consists of alumni, educators, corporate managers, and community leaders. You may choose to include your fee schedule, but why not include a note about providing discounts for nonprofit and educational groups?

Offer to prepare a press release prior to a presentation. If you craft it, it will contain all pertinent information; otherwise, you're leaving it to chance if the program committee people have their hands at it. You can attach a black and white 3 x 5 camera-ready print to the news release. Add your name and address on the back of the photo so that it will be returned. Sometimes newspapers will have the space to run an accompanying photo of the speaker.

Design a promotional brochure. Develop a name and tagline for yourself or your company, such as "LYN JONES: Motivational Presentations for Conferences and Meetings," complete with a photo and a visual graphic or logo on the front. Inside include the topics you can address. The more broad, the better, so that you don't need to revise the brochure often or feel locked into one set of topics. Give examples of audiences that you've addressed, such as the Rotary Club, chamber of commerce, the Businesswomen's Association, Christmas Cheer Kickoff Campaign Dinner, and the 2002 Alumni Reunion of University of "Greenstowne." Incorporate quotes from satisfied clients.

Develop a website with photos of yourself at a podium or shown interacting with a lively group. If resources allow, include streaming video so that your web-readers can see you in action. The website will market your services internationally and is a good investment for the ambitious speaker. Include a list of presentation topics as bullet points, and highlight possible topics for a keynote address that could be the centerpiece of a conference or annual meeting.

As a keynote speaker, you will set the tone and give a broad overview of a critical issue that links to the conference theme, increasing interest and providing a context for the meeting or other presentations. The keynote speaker charges more than the average presenter because she is known to

216 ● *Women Seen and Heard*

have personal charisma, a list of reputable clients, and/or celebrity status. The client expects keynoters to be capable of inspiring others to be creative or fight the good fight, and this is a valuable service to the client.

Are you an "expert" on your subject or in your field? Promote your expertise to the media. Reporters may need a quote from someone with your background or credentials. Include specific topics that you can address. Enroll in a media association that lists "experts." Keep a record of your radio and television interviews and press clippings. If you keep your knowledge base current and are easy to work with, you may be the first person a reporter calls.

Preparation and Organization Saves Time

Prepare a list of topics, both broad and general, that reflect your expertise and interests. Find your audience. Then, just the way that builders can construct a mobile home in sections beforehand using modular construction, organize your materials into modules that can stand alone or be integrated into longer presentations. If you're passionate about children's health, the modules can involve "funding issues," "statistics," "social policy," "parents role," "innovative programs," "cultural differences," and "the role of schools." Each of these modules includes key points with sub-points, quotes, statistics, and visual aids. When an unexpected opportunity arises, you can pull out one or several file folders on the subject organized by "module," and be ready to go in no time.

As a woman presenter, you won't want your presentation to be dry or dull. Find the heart of the matter and connect personally with each point by sharing relevant and personal anecdotes wherever you can.

Prepare clean and simple worksheets for your audiences. Handouts can include such provocative questions as:

- *If you had the power to make a change regarding the issue we are discussing today, what would you do?*
- *Which action can you take in your present situation or position?*
- *Whom could you recruit to assist you in this process?*
- *What would you say in your recruiting pitch?*

Your presentation can help the audience answer these questions.

If you want your audience to contact representatives, then provide a resource list. If your talk was based on several new resources, you might want to provide audience members with a bibliography and a list of additional resources. If your references are controversial, you can provide the source material in a handout. As a professional, you'll want to make sure that your logo, name, and contact information are on each page with the date of the presentation. This information helps people remember you later. Satisfied audiences are the best referral networks. Everything you say, do, and distribute helps you to be seen and heard by potential clients.

Ensure That You Are Introduced As a Pro

If the speaker is introduced well, the audience will react with excitement, anticipating what they are about to hear. The right introduction will create open minds in the audience members. You can leave their reaction to chance or take control of the situation. See the sample we have provided as an example of how a speaker might be introduced:

Sample Introduction:

It's tough to be successful in today's uncertain world. Competing for customer attention in a global market-

place means facing constant scrutiny by people of different backgrounds, values, and needs. When you're in a leadership role, you need to make decisions quickly, some of which will inevitably be unpopular. Our speaker today has the kind of wisdom that allowed her to navigate through stormy seas and bring her small agency to great success.

Jane Gonzalez brings her expertise to us today in not one but several areas. First, she was an amateur athlete who made it into the 1990 Olympics as a marathon swimmer. Her discipline and belief in herself stood her in good stead over the years as she developed a second and more recently a third career.

Second, Dr. Gonzalez is also an educator. She's been a principal of an inner city school and college teacher, training teachers for challenging urban school environments. Her textbooks on teacher education are widely used, and her commentaries about the state of education can often be heard on Public Radio.

Third, she was recently appointed to head a public agency designed to unclog our freeways. She believes in developing and promoting alternative transportation systems that will be cost effective and user-friendly for everyone, including children, teens, and seniors.

Jane is not only someone with ambitious career plans, but also a parent who understands the juggling act facing many of us. Today she'll discuss how improving transportation is everybody's business. We have much to learn from her. Please welcome Jane Gonzalez.

Aren't you eager to hear from Jane after that introduction? The introduction has already enhanced her credibility as the voice of authority. What information about **your** background would create anticipation in the minds and hearts of your audience? Write your own introduction. Ask a close friend to write one for you. Then compare them. Any surprises?

Writing a wonderful introduction and having it read wonderfully are two different things. Many speakers think of a way to ensure that the introduction you wrote is actually read by the appropriate program chairperson. It often doesn't work that way, because of the human dynamics and unexpected events that inevitably occur on the day of the program. Here's one idea we found helpful for taking control. Prior to the event, in a conversation with the program chair, consider saying:

Sally, I'm recording this presentation and would like to have your voice heard introducing me. Could you read this paragraph for me, and tell me if you're comfortable with it?

After she reads it, thank her and tell her, "That was great! Could you read it just that way tomorrow?" Nevertheless, you should still be prepared for unexpected changes in the schedule that may cause this prepared text to be scrapped in the interest of time, with a comment such as "You can read all about our speaker's qualifications in the program notes." At least, you'll know you've tried!

There are many aspects of a professional practice as a public speaker, from the fee structure, marketing and promoting tasks, cultivating relationships with your clients, or becoming a paid spokesperson for one organization. Giving presentations and speeches in your public voice gets easier as you go. Each prepared set of slides, handouts, quotes, and statistics can be the building block for the next presentation. And because it will take less time to prepare for each subsequent presentation, you can focus on the idiosyncratic needs of the next audience. Each presentation can be embellished with current anecdotes and news stories.

After you've performed to the satisfaction of your clients, you will find yourself in high demand. Your reputation will lead to new speaking engagements, specifically through client referrals. When the mike is on and the podium is lit, it will be your turn to be paid to be seen and heard.

LESSON
*You can prepare yourself for a career as a paid,
professional speaker.*

Section Five
APPENDIX

Women Today—Facts and Figures

Social Demographics

Changes in social demographics require that diverse women are seen and heard in leadership roles.

Women, who are 52 percent of California's voters, constitute only 40 percent of the membership of city, county, and state commissions today. Still, that is an improvement. Women's service on city commissions increased from 35.5 percent to 39.8 percent, from 34.3 percent to 38.5 percent on county commissions, and from 27.6 percent to 34.4 percent at the state level since 1980.

The median age has increased from thirty-one to thirty-four years old. Women are "older" today as a group than they were in 1980. The number of teens and young adults declined, while the number of middle-aged and older women increased. More women are older than men. Women account for 51 percent of the total population, but become an increasing majority after age twenty-five and comprise 55 percent of people aged forty-five and older.

Women are having children later in life: in 1990 there were 4,158,212 babies born in the U.S., the highest reported since 1962, near the end of the Baby Boom era. In 1990 the fertility rate for women ages thirty to thirty-four was the highest it has been in the past two decades, and thirty-five to thirty-nine has increased more than any other age group. Birthrates for girls fifteen to seventeen were up 157 percent.

However, more women now live in households without children than with them.

At first glance, women have benefited from the advent of birth control technology and the Roe v. Wade Supreme Court decision that made reproductive choice a woman's decision, but

the issue of abortion is controversial and, some say, as divisive a national issue as slavery was. On March 17, 2003, in a final triumph for abortion foes, the Senate rejected a second attempt to substitute a ban on abortions after the fetus is viable outside the mother. That proposal included exceptions for the life and health of the mother, and failed, 60–35.[89]

Supporters of the bill attacked the controversial ("partial birth") procedure as barbaric and opponents said the measure was the opening salvo of a larger assault on abortion rights. Abortion rights supporters have pledged a court challenge. "This bill is unconstitutional," argued Senator Barbara Boxer, D-California, citing the lack of an exemption in cases where the health of the mother is in jeopardy. "This will get legislation past Congress, but the Supreme Court will have the final say," CBS News Legal Analyst Andrew Cohen reports.

When we look at the future, we know that households will continue to look very different from the way they did in 1980. Women, a particularly high proportion of whom are African American, head one in nine households. One in six 'never-married' women have given birth.

Women's sex roles are expanding to include the role of breadwinner. Even young girls are imagining themselves as mothers and workers employed outside the home. Commenting on the 1999 annual Roper study that was based on a nationwide cross section of 1,214 six to seventeen-year-old children, researcher and Vice President Peter Silsbee said that he was "surprised to learn how many girls see themselves as breadwinners," while at the same time retaining traditional aspirations. In their minds, they expect that as women they will play both roles.

Silsbee said that although twice as many girls as boys (52 percent to 25 percent) envisioned staying home to raise their children, it was notable that a full quarter of the boys even considered child-rearing an option, "further signaling the erosion of sharply divided gender responsibilities." Fifty-five percent of girls and 45 percent of boys expected to arrange day care, a finding the researchers said reflected the primary child-rearing responsibilities that women still bear even as part of the work force.[90]

Nearly 80 percent of U.S. women now live in metropolitan—as opposed to suburban or rural—areas. Increasing numbers of women live outside what has been considered the typical American household, which consist of a married couple with children, including older women who are "empty nesters." An unprecedented 13.5 million women, roughly one in seven, lived alone in 1990.

Living a longer life makes each woman increasingly likely to spend time in various types of households. Examples include living alone before or after marriage, or living with a spouse long after her children have grown. Women are getting married later, the divorce rate remains high, and more women are having children without being married. All these factors affect the variety of women's lifestyles. Mother-child subfamilies (families living in someone else's house) are a majority in every racial/ethnic group except Asian-Americans, where a female heads one of four subfamilies.

One can't generalize about marriage being the natural or most desired state for all women in contemporary America. Later marriages, more divorces, and greater life expectancy

mean that an increasing share of adult women are not currently married, and that, due to the high rate of divorce, women are spending more of their lives unmarried. Although married women are still the majority, a higher proportion of today's younger women will remain single throughout their lives. (The exception to this is African Americans.) There was a dramatic increase in the proportion of never-married women in late '20s to early '30s and, since 1980, an increase in divorced and widowed women.

More women will be alone in their old age. As the Baby Boom generation ages, a larger share of older women may also lack adult children to help them, as many had smaller families or remained childless.[91]

Poor women and single parents continue to live in substandard housing, where their children are subjected to criminal behavior and have access to drugs and poor schools. Although women have difficulty purchasing homes on their own, once women have adequate resources, they do what it takes to make the commitment. In fact, according to a year 2000 National Association of Realtors report, "rising incomes helped single females account for 20 percent of all home purchases last year, nearly twice the level a few years ago."[92]

Private Sector Demographics

Women's lack of career advancement in the private sector require that women become more effective in asserting their capacity for leadership.

The perpetuation of well-documented sexist stereotypes and biases against women by male decision-makers remains serious. Women CEO's still make about sixty-eight cents to the dollar compared to men's compensation for the same position.[93] Barriers to upward mobility may jeopardize

women's health, as indicated in the famous Framingham Heart Study, which showed an increased incidence of coronary heart disease among clerical workers.[94]

Where the gap remains enormous is between entering a profession and rising to a top decision-making leadership position. The *landscape*, not the hilltop, is what is changing. The Federal Glass Ceiling Commission Bipartisan Study in 1995 found that the "glass ceiling" that prevents women from rising to the top of corporate America was essentially intact.

According to Patricia O'Brien, dean of Simmons College Graduate School of Management, women in business avoid the feminist label because it brands them as troublemakers and whiners, even though women comprise only 2 percent of senior management. "Women still need particular skills to succeed. We still play by men's rules."[95] Nearly half of employed women are in lower-paying administrative support and service jobs.

When it comes to the future, women are not as likely to be involved in leadership roles within the Information Age economy as men are. The Information Technology Association of America, a trade group, estimates a shortfall of about 346,000 computer professionals this year. In spite of this favorable job market, the proportion of women among U.S. computer professionals has fallen in the 1990s—from 35.4 percent to 29.1 percent of that workforce—according to the Bureau of Labor Statistics.

The under-representation of women is particularly pronounced at the top-tier computer schools, such as UC Berkeley and Carnegie Mellon, which feed the elite industry jobs. The Educational Testing Service reports that last year only 17 percent of high school students taking advanced placement tests in computer science were girls—by far the lowest percentage of any subject.[96] This means women who

are already in the computer science field need to develop public speaking skills and become more outspoken, thus becoming more visible examples of what pioneering women can achieve in a male dominated field.

Many of the projects and tools in the computer industry are not formatted for women. Even with training in the field, many women are faced with a lack of role models, and performance pressure is high. Some high-tech companies work hard to recruit and retain female professionals, hoping to buck the trend, but they have met only limited success. For example, at Microsoft, women make up 16 percent of technical professionals, and the proportion of women in those jobs at Intel has been stalled at about 25 percent since 1993. What leadership role will women play in the high-tech world that is so critical to our economy?

On the positive side, women-owned businesses are booming. As of 1999, there are 9.1 million in the U.S., accounting for 38 percent of all businesses in the country that employ 27.5 million people and generate $3.6 trillion in sales, according to the National Foundation for Women Business Owners. According to the U.S. Department of Labor, within a few years half of all businesses will have a female owner.[97] Employer's tolerance for sexism may be declining, particularly when it draws press attention. When journalist Jimmy Breslin burst out of his office at New York *Newsday* and spouted off sexist and racist invectives against an Asian-American colleague, *Newsday* suspended him for two weeks without pay.[98] Women's economic power indicates that they have new opportunities for being seen and heard. On a panel about the future of publishing, one panelist from Oregon who owns a car dealership said: "Make your newspapers more appealing to women.... Women now make up 40 percent of all new car buyers."[99]

Public Sector Demographics

Women are becoming increasingly aware of the need to participate in policy discussions and to be taken seriously as a voting force. For example, women account for half the American population, yet only thirteen senators and sixty congresswomen represent us,[100] and there remains no constitutional amendment guaranteeing women equal rights. There are only seven female governors, of Arizona, Delaware, Kansas, Hawaii, Michigan, Montana and Puerto Rico.

A Gallup poll in the mid 1980s already indicated "Women are seeing a direct connection between policy decisions and their own lives, and are choosing to become increasingly active politically, especially at state and local levels." Women have been the voting majority in every major U.S. election since 1964, and can provide the swing votes in a national election, as they did in the 1996 election for president with the largest gender gap in American history.[101]

A majority 2000 survey of American women conducted by *Good Housekeeping* magazine and women.com indicated that women voters share common ground and that, although their spouses are their most important political influence, women surveyed believe that they vote with their heads, not with their hearts.[102]

Women face problems of violence that are stunning in scope. The San Francisco Police Department receives approximately ten thousand calls for assistance due to family/domestic violence per year. Family violence is the leading cause of all solved homicides for women.[104] According to National Statistics collected by the Bureau of Justice, the FBI and Uniform Crime Reports in 1995:

◆ Men committed 95 percent of all documented domestic assaults against women.

- Every fifteen seconds a woman is battered, resulting in more than ninety murders each week.

- Thirty-one percent of women in this country reported physical abuse by a husband or boyfriend at some time during their lives.

- Four million women per year require medical attention or police intervention.

- Each year, one-third of women who are victimized are battered repeatedly or are hurt by "serial victimization."

- Forty-seven percent of the husbands who beat their wives do so three or more times a year.

- Seventeen percent of adult pregnant women are battered.

- The number of teenagers (thirteen to nineteen years old) who are battered during pregnancy may be as high as 21 percent.

Domestic violence is the most underreported crime in the United States.

Educational Demographics

In terms of education, more women are high school dropouts than are college graduates. However, did you know that more women than men are going to college and earning baccalaureate degrees? The numbers of women and men in medical school and law school are almost equal. When it comes to academic employment, however, even the most elite universities have low percentages of tenured faculty who are women: 13.8 percent at Yale, 13.3 percent at Stanford, and 11.5 percent at Harvard, as of 1997.[105]

A field that guarantees greater likelihood of employment, like Computer Science, is lacking women's participation.

Women comprise about 15–20 percent of the student body of computer sciences[106] which amounts to approximately a 5 percent gain over a decade. This may seem too small a step, but it is a step in the right direction. There are new educational outreach programs designed to help girls transcend the attitudinal barriers that lead most women to choose certain conventional professions and to remove institutional barriers to females entering into the fields of science, engineering, and computer studies.

While most agree that the system is flawed, given the scope of the problems that face chronically unemployed individuals, inter-institutional partnerships between employers and educational programs have demonstrated creative efforts to meet a wide range of needs, including opportunities for young and re-entry women to enter non-traditional career paths and organizational pipelines designed for upward mobility.

Changes have occurred on the sports fields of America's schools as a result of women advocating for equality. Over the past two decades, women have won equal opportunity legislation such as Title IX that requires equal access to athletic programs. Women's success in soccer on the international scene has emerged from such groundbreaking legislation, and girls today have new athletic heroes. We've all seen front page pictures of Brandy Chastain after a victorious soccer match. Interestingly, younger tennis players are often ignorant of the legislation that gave them equal access to competitive sports and allowed them to achieve great success and the celebrity that men have achieved. Legislation is being proposed to challenge the legality of Title IX as it affects those sports that have typically been thought of as played by men only: football, wrestling, and basketball. The final vote at the January 2003 meeting of the Commission on Opportunity in

Athletics conveyed "more concern with what men had lost than with what women never had. . . . When it comes to Title IX, everyone knows it's still better to be a man."[107]

Ethnic Demographics

Diverse women need to assert their ideas, opinions, and proposals for action in public forums and become appointed and elected officials, and more successful in the business world.

Given the demographic changes that have occurred in the late '90s, men's rules do not fully encompass the needs of increasingly diverse women who comprise the American population. Who is the American woman today? Research by the State Department's Interagency on Women indicates that the demographic changes are shifting in dramatic ways that are creating new issues to be grappled with. In order to address these emerging issues, leaders will need to question the assumptions being made about women and their lifestyles, from cradle to grave. No longer can we stereotype "women's issues" as those that would only be of concern to white, middle-class women.

American women are more racially and ethnically diverse than before and more diverse than men; 30.7 million women are members of an ethnic or racial minority group—that's nearly one in four women. Few elected or appointed officials, however, are women of color.

More women are foreign-born; for example, 8 percent of the total female population, or 10.1 million girls, were born outside the U.S. Nearly half of Hispanic women who are ages eighteen to sixty-four are immigrants, as are four out of five Asian-American women. There is an increase in the number of women without a fundamental knowledge of English;

almost four million (3 percent of all U.S. women) live in linguistic isolation where no one over age thirteen speaks English fluently; Spanish is the first language for most of these women.[108]

On almost every aspect of advancement opportunities, women of color are significantly behind other women who work in nontraditional jobs, have access to higher education, and have a broader array of lifestyle choices. Recent data on diversity in the military, however, provided some reasons for optimism. For example, although Blacks and women tend to receive initial assignments that give their careers "a slow start" and have limited their access to peer and mentor networks, a report on promotion rates showed that women have made considerable progress in comparison to Blacks in the military, going from under 6 percent of the officer corps twenty years ago to more that 14 percent today.[109]

The Working Woman

In the old days, one myth was that women worked for "pin money." Working women who support themselves and their families need to challenge these "myths" by participating in the policy debates that will affect their economic self-sufficiency and advancement. The chances are greater than 99 percent that all women will work in their lifetimes, whether by choice or chance, reflecting a remarkable increase in the proportion of mothers who work. This is a result of changes in the attitudes of society toward working moms and the desires of women themselves, as well as inflation, recession, falling wages, divorce, and spousal unemployment.

It's only fair that women be paid equitably with men in comparable roles. Although governmental agencies have adopted 'comparable worth' protocols, distinct gaps remain in the private sector. In high tech companies, the fastest growing sector of the economy, women are a small percentage of technical professionals. For every dollar that men earn, women earn anywhere from sixty-eight to eighty cents for the same work, depending upon their occupational role. Although educated younger women are faring better than older women, the proportion of women among U.S. computer professionals actually fell about six percentage points in the '90s.[110]

Only 2 percent of U.S. corporate chief executive officers are women, and women hold only one in ten seats on the boards of Fortune 500 companies. In 1999, women held 11.2 percent of total board seats on Fortune 500 companies, up slightly from 11.1 percent the prior year. 419 of the Fortune 500 companies (or 84 percent) have one or more women directors, down 2 percent since 1998 when there were 429 such companies (or 86 percent).[111]

A recent resource study by Korn/Ferry International and Catalyst found that 95 percent of senior level managers—vice presidents and above—are men, while only 5 percent of senior managers are women.[112] As for the U.S. military, only thirty-seven women are active duty generals or admirals.[113] Why aren't educated, trained, and experienced women moving forward?

Although women have become a majority of professional workers, they are continuing to juggle many roles; specifically, we know that approximately one-half of mothers of young children also work outside the home. By contrast, the responsibilities of work and home life have changed little for married men. An American Association of University Women (AAUW) research project indicates that childcare is a core problem for working women because society believes caring for the children is the mother's problem, even in a two-parent family or when two incomes are required to sustain the family.[114] Progressive companies, agencies, and some institutions are finally exploring ways to provide on-site childcare. Those employers who took initiative to meet the need quickly came to realize the positive impact on worker loyalty and increased productivity. Still, the corporate efforts to meet the need for childcare programs are 'a drop in the proverbial bucket.' Continued advocacy is essential.

Sexual harassment continues to be a problem as women move into formerly all-male fields and professions. A 1996 survey of California companies showed that sexual harassment complaints, especially complaints of verbal harassment, had increased almost 50 percent in two years. A survey of executives in the hospitality industry revealed that sexual harassment is one of their greatest concerns.

Sexual harassment claims are said to be on the rise in the financial services industry as well, and awards to victims of harassment in that industry can add up to six figures. In 1990, the Equal Employment Opportunity Commission (EEOC) received just over 6,000 sexual harassment complaints. The number of complaints has steadily risen, and in 1995 and 1996, the agency logged over 15,000 complaints.

In recent years, companies have recognized that sexual harassment is a serious business issue. They have acknowledged what women have known all along: sexual harassment isn't about sex. It isn't about romance . . . (or) flirtation. It *is* about the abuse of authority.

Sexual harassment is not confined to male-dominated jobs or to blue collar workers, nor is it limited to sexual overtures from the boss. Women in all industries and at all levels say that they have experienced sexual harassment from coworkers, from customers, and from vendors. Women who experience sexual harassment can suffer the same depression, anguish, guilt, fear, and powerlessness as those who are assaulted or raped. Yet, many women hesitate to report harassment, and some never do. They fail to come forward because they fear retaliation, that they won't be believed, that the harassment will escalate, or that they can't prove a case. They also fail to come forward because they think the harassment is their fault or fear an invasion of privacy.[115]

How can we ensure that research related to women's health is adequately funded? Activists and advocates have worked with corporations and individuals to sponsor events that will increase funding for breast and ovarian cancer research outside of government sources. Clinical trials need to use women as part of their studies, and as more women move into decision-making positions in this industry, research can be more equitable.

The cost of healthcare is rising and yet insurance costs are beyond the reach of many. The average cost of nursing home care in the United States in 1995 was $37,000 a year, over $100 per day. Medicare, designed to protect us in later years from big medical expenses, pays for nursing home and home care only in certain limited and very specific circumstances. When it comes to financing long-term care in this country, you are, in short, on your own, unless you become impoverished to the point of qualifying for Medicaid, but this welfare program is now threatened with large funding cuts. Long-term care insurance is of special importance to women. Women are much more likely than men to need nursing home care. It is estimated that the majority of women (one-third of men) reaching the age of 60 will need nursing home care before they die.[116] This is probably because older women are much more likely to be single than men and because women more readily take on personal care of their spouses. In addition, women survive longer on average after admission to the nursing home.[117]

Final Comment

Although this is a brave new "post-modern," and some would say "post-feminist" world, most Americans assume that women's roles have changed dramatically for the better; however, our institutions haven't accommodated women's emerging needs for new social policies that support their desire to be successful. And the changes that are needed to make our lives better as women affect everyone. We need to hear from people like you or your friends who have a new social vision that allows us to function effectively within a global, multicultural and high-technology world, one that provides equal rights, equal access, and equal opportunities for women.

All ideas are good ideas, at least to start the discussion and necessary debates. And leaders are people who have a new vision of the future, and their proposals for change start the ball rolling. As a function of the leadership role, public speaking is one way of persuading lawmakers and employers to change outdated policies. Then again, women can change things for the better by becoming lawyers, policymakers, and employers, as many are trying to do. In new leadership roles, women will be required to speak effectively to groups and audiences in many different settings both in and outside of courtrooms and boardrooms. We hope that this book will assist each woman reader to gain credibility as the voice of authority, whether she speaks to a small group or a large audience.

Women Seen and Heard
Biographies

Susan Lowell Butler, a senior non-profit association executive with special expertise in communications, community organizing and management, joined the Coalition for America's Children as its first staff member in July 1996. Ms. Butler is responsible for development and implementation of the Coalition's "Who's for Kids and Who's Just Kidding" Voter Education Campaign, designed to make children's issues a visible and important part of presidential campaigns. Before joining the Coalition, Ms. Butler was the chief executive officer of two national non-profit organizations, the National Women's Hall of Fame and Women in Communications, Inc. An ovarian and breast cancer survivor, Ms. Butler is a health-care writer who recently wrote a website on cancer pain. She serves on the NCI Director's Consumer Liaison Group and the NIH Clinical Center Patient Advisory Committee, and is a peer reviewer for NCI. Ms. Butler is a founding member of the Alliance and the Ovarian Cancer Coalition of Greater Washington.

Liz Carpenter is a well-known writer and lecturer with a lifetime of political reporting an active participation on the national scene from which to draw. Walter Cronkite said of her, "Liz Carpenter is much more than an American original; she is an American and a Texas original. Her inside stories of our nation's political life over the last half century are priceless." Her first hand knowledge as an insider and confidant in the nation's capitol covers nine presidents from Roosevelt to Bush, three of whom named her to positions of trust. After eighteen years as a Washington correspondent covering the Capitol and White House, she served as Vice President Lyndon

B. Johnson's executive assistant, and later became press secretary and staff director to Lady Bird Johnson. She also served in appointed positions in the administrations of Gerald Ford, Jimmy Carter, and Bill Clinton.

Congresswoman Loretta Sanchez was elected to Congress in November 1996 to represent the 46th Congressional District of California. Congresswoman Sanchez is a member of the National Security Committee and the Committee on Education and the Workforce. She serves on various boards, which include the Pepperdine University Hispanic Advisory Council and the National Society of Hispanic MBAs. In 1995, Congresswoman Sanchez incorporated KinderCaminata, a program introducing kindergartners from low-income school districts to their local community college. Last March, over 10,000 kindergartners throughout Orange County spent the day at a community college with their parents. Previous to her congressional service, Congresswoman Sanchez was a businesswoman in Santa Ana specializing in assistance to public agencies regarding financial matters.

Ann Stone is an activist and advocate for women. Active in Politics since age twelve, Ann has worked in over three hundred campaigns as everything from precinct worker to campaign manager to actual candidate.

In fundraising, she has set records in the past for most money raised for Congress (still unbroken) and for the Senate. When Ann Stone first went out on her own in business in March 1982, she set out not only to be a financial success in the direct response marketing industry, but to use her experience to find ways to create a platform for the discussion and dissemination of information of importance to women. As a first step towards success in March 1988—just six years later—her first company was named one of the top direct response marketing agencies in the country. Motivated by a desire to provide greater access to credit for female entrepreneurs, Ann has gone on to found three other companies and helped launch a national bank.

In late 1989, she decided to launch a national political group, "Republicans For Choice" (RFC) in order to locate and motivate the majority in the Republican Party who are pro-choice, change the Party platform and elect pro-choice Republicans at the federal, state, and local levels. In 1996 she was one of the first three original incorporators of the National Museum of Women's History, upon whose board she now sits. Ann also is a regular panel member in the PBS commentary show "To the Contrary."

Janice Weinman, Ph.D. is the corporate vice-president of External Affairs for Mount Sinai NYU Health, where she is responsible for marketing, communications, and public relations for the five hospitals making up Mount Sinai NYU Health. Formerly the executive director of the American Association of University Women, one of the oldest and largest national organizations of women, Dr. Weinman was the chief executive officer of three corporations that promote education and equity for women and girls.

Dr. Weinman serves on various boards including: Visiting Committee, Harvard University Graduate School of Education; Board of Directors, the Council on Basic Education; Vice President, Jewish Community Relations Council of New York; Member, Women's Leadership Board, John F. Kennedy School of Government, Harvard University; and Founding Member, Board of Directors, Hadassah Foundation. She is a regular keynote speaker, panelist, and workshop leader at national conferences on higher, elementary and secondary education, community development, and organizational growth and development.

Marie Wilson is in her thirteenth year as president of the Ms. Foundation for Women. An activist, author, and expert on the issues that affect the lives of women and their families, Ms. Wilson has acted as the leader of the only national multi-issue women's fund in the United States, increasing the annual budget from $400,000 to $6.2 million and raising the foundation's $10 million endowment fund. She co-created the successful public education campaign, *Take Our Daughters To Work Day* and co-founded *The*

White House Project in 1998 to get more women elected to office, including the presidency. In 1999, she founded *The Women's Leadership Fund,* a public education initiative dedicated to changing perceptions about and biases against women's leadership ability.

Betsy Meyers serves as director of President Clinton's Welfare to Work Initiative at the Small Business Administration. Ms. Meyers serves a significant role as facilitator of the president's welfare to work program, evaluating and developing the most effective strategy for involving small business in this new initiative. Before joining the Small Business Administration, Ms. Meyers served as director of the White House Office of Women's Outreach. While serving at the White House, Ms. Meyers worked as the president's top advisor on women's issues, serving as a liaison between public and private women's organizations and the Clinton Administration. She is now director of alumni relations for the John F. Kennedy School of Government at Harvard University.

Ida Castro was nominated by President Clinton as director of the Women's Bureau at the Department of Labor in August 1996. Prior to this, Ms. Castro served as acting deputy solicitor of Labor and the deputy assistant secretary for the Office of Worker's Compensation. During her three-year tenure at the Department of Labor, Ms. Castro received three vice presidential awards ("The Hammer Awards") for innovative approaches that streamlined government, improved customer services and reduced taxpayers burden. Prior her federal service, Ms. Castro practiced health/labor/employment law and was an associate professor at Rutgers University.

Kathleen Drennan, Chair for Advancement of Women's Health president of Drennan Healthcare International (DHI), Kathleen Drennan established her company to provide strategic guidance to pharmaceutical, academic, and other research organizations looking to bridge the gap between good science and cost-effective business principles within the clinical trials and medical research industry. She is a speaker at conferences on the subject of women's health care issues. Drennan also sits on the advisory board of directors, eHealthcareWorld.

Laura Groppe, CEO/President of Girl Games, Inc. Laura spent seven years as a co-producer and assistant director in the entertainment business winning an Academy Award in 1992 for Best Short Film, the Best Cinematography award at the 1994 Sundance Film Festival and four MTV music video awards in 1994. That same year, Laura left Hollywood to return to Texas to launch Girl Games, Inc. Comprised of a Research Lab, Studio and Planetgirl.com, a research tool and online community for girls. Girl Games focuses on researching the teen girl demographic and helping businesses make intelligent decisions concerning the Generation-Y female consumer.

Ms. Groppe currently serves on corporate advisory boards and is a board member on Planet 10, a NASA-supported program dedicated to promoting girls in science. She is a committed philanthropist, supporting organizations such as the Susan Komen Foundation in the fight against breast cancer, and SMARTgirls, a non-profit organization committed to mentoring and training girls in technology.

Geraldine Jensen, Founder and President of Association for Children for Enforcement of Support Inc. When Geraldine's marriage to James Jensen failed, she was a single parent struggling to support the family. She returned to school and became a Licensed Practical Nurse, trying to work overtime so that her sons had the opportunity to attend Catholic school and participate in sports. Unfortunately, she became ill and ended up on welfare for a second time. In March of 1984, she walked into the county child support agency and demanded assistance with collection of the now almost $12,000 due in back child support. The prosecutor assigned to her case told her, "I'm so tired of you women coming in here, whining and complaining about child support, if you think you can do a better job go and do it!" Geraldine left his office an went to the local newspaper and placed an ad that said, "Need Child Support? Call me." The response was positive and she soon founded ACES, *The Association for Children For Enforcement of Support*. As executive director, she gained media coverage—including a television film about the issue and her achievements—and focused public attention on the difficulty of enforcing child support payments from absentee dads, and new enforcement laws were passed.

Delaine Eastin, a native Californian, received her bachelor's degree from the University of California, Davis, and a master's degree in political science from the University of California, Santa Barbara. She taught political science and women's studies for seven years, and then served as a corporate planner for Pacific Telesis Group. Before being elected to the California State Assembly in 1986, Eastin was a member of the City Council in Union City and the Alameda County Library Advisory Commission. Ms. Eastin was elected to the California State Assembly in 1986. After four terms in the California State Assembly, she was the first woman to be elected California's State Superintendent of Public Instruction. In that role, she is a member of the Board of Regents of the University of California, the Trustees of the California State Colleges and University, and the California Education Round Table, all of which require public communication skills.

As an ardent spokesperson for school libraries and because she has persistently worked to improve libraries for the 12 percent of America's school children who attend California schools, she was awarded The Crystal Apple Award. She has received the Distinguished Alumni Award from the University of California, Santa Barbara; the Woman of Achievement Award from the Women's Fund; and the Leader Award from California Leadership, the Faculty Association of California Community Colleges, the American Business Women's Association, Soroptimists International, and many business and professional organizations.

Footnotes

Section One
Chapter 2

1   Robin Tolmach Lakoff, *Talking Power: The Politics of Language* (New York: Basic Books, 1990), 206.

2   David Wallechinsky and Amy Wallace, *The Book of Lists* (New York: Little Brown and Company, 1993).

3   Sheila Murphy, "Podiumitis (An Extremely Common, Though Rarely Discussed Affliction)," *Santa Barbara News Press* 29 Aug. 1999: J–1.

4   Barbara Ehrenreich, "Public Freaking," *Ms.*, Sept. 1989: 40–41.

5   Jenny Allen, "Conquering Fear," *Real Simple* Nov. 2001: 103–105.

6   Pauline Clance and Suzanne Imes, "The Impostor Phenomenon Among High Achieving Women: Dynamics and Therapeutic Intervention," *Psychotherapy Theory, Research and Practice* 15 (1978): 241–247.

7   Jamieson, Kathleen Hall, *Eloquence in an Electronic Age: The Transformation of Political Speechmaking* (New York: Oxford University Press, 1988). Beyond the Double Bind: Women in Leadership (New York: Oxford University Press, 1995).

8   See Appendix for changing demographics that describe the issues facing women as they seek to be successful.

9   Ellen Goodman, "Of Pants Suits and Glass Ceilings," Boston Globe as seen in the *Santa Barbara News Press* 7 Nov 2002: A–13.

10 Jane Ciabattari, "Women Who Could Be President," *Parade* 7 Feb 1999: 7.

11 Bridge, M.J. (1993) *The News: Looking like America? Not yet . . . New York: Women, Men, and Media* as referenced in Matlin, p.41–43.

12 Tolmach Lakoff, 208–209.

13 Rhoda Unger and Mary Crawford, *Women and Gender: A Feminist Psychology* (New York: McGraw Hill, 1996): 241.

14   Tolmach Lakoff, 204.

15   Nancy M. Henley, *Body Politics: Power, Sex, and Nonverbal Communication* (New York: Simon and Schuster, Inc., 1977).

16   Mark Knapp, *Nonverbal Communication in Human Interaction*, (New York: Holt, Rinehart & Winston, 1978).

Section Two
Chapter 3

17   Terence Samuel, "Portrait: Nancy Pelosi, She's Cracking the Whip," *U.S. News and World Report*, 17 June 2002: 18–19.

18   "Women on the Hill," *Outlook* 92.3 (Fall 1998).

19   Testimony of Rep. Barbara Jordan before the House Judiciary Committee, July 25, 1974. This information was found at http://www.watergate.info/impeachment/74-07-25_barbara-jordan.html and viewed on 20 Jan. 03.

20   Barbara Ehrenreich quoted in Elizabeth Kay, "The Face of Power," *Working Woman*, Oct 1993: 50.

21   Gail Sheehy, *Hillary's Choice*, (New York: Random House, 1999): 261–262.

22   Marion Wright Edelman, Speech at Howard University, Washington, D.C., 12 May 1990.

23   http://www.utexas.edu/lbj/. Use the search engine to find information on Barbara Jordan. This website was reviewed on 20 Jan. 2003.

24   Hillary Clinton, Women.Future@Harvard, Kennedy School of Government, Harvard University, 5 Apr. 2000.

25   This quote was found on the following website, quoting Ann Richards' speech at the 1988 Democratic Convention, http://gos.sbc.edu/r/richards.html. This site was reviewed for accuracy on 18 Feb. 2003.

26   http://www.house.gov/lee/, reviewed on 20 Jan. 2003. Website for The Office of Congresswoman Barbara Lee representing the Ninth District of California of California. Search the text of her votes.

27   Hillary Clinton, Senate Debate in Manhattan, NBC News, 8 Oct. 2000.

28   From an interview with Susan Lowell Butler, Former Director of National Women's Hall of Fame, National Women's Political Caucus Convention, Houston, Texas, August 1997.

Chapter 4

29   Robert L. Jackson, "Women to Get $508 Million for Job Bias by U.S. Agency," *Los Angles Times* 23 Mar 2000: A1.

30   Margaret W. Matlin, *The Psychology of Women* (Texas: Harcourt Brace College Publishers, 1996): 219–228.

31   http://www.tsl.state.tx.us/. This is the website for the Texas State Library Archives Commission. Search for "Ann Richards" to gain access to an information network about her life.

32   Interview with former Press Secretary Liz Carpenter (Johnson administration), National Women's Political Caucus Convention, Houston, Texas, August 1997.

33   Interview, Liz Carpenter, 1997.

34   Peggy Noonan, *What I Saw at the Revolution: A Political Life in the Reagan Era* (New York: Ballantine Books, 1990).

35   Interview with Geraldine Jensen, Houston, Texas, NWPC Convention, 1997

36   Tony Perry, "Whatever Happened to 'the Year of the Woman?,'" *Los Angeles Times*, 20 Nov 1995: A1,5.

37   *Time* Dec. 2002.

Section Three
Chapter 5

38   Interview with Susan Lowell Butler, former executive director of National Women's Hall of Fame, Women in Communications, Coalition for America's Children and advocate for ovarian cancer research

39   J.D. Zahniser, And Then She Said . . . : Quotations by Women for Every Occasion, 2nd Ed. (St. Paul; Caillech Press, 1995), 10.

40   Kedric Francis, "Women CEO's: Leading Business to the Future," *OC Metro* 15 July 1999: 34–42.

41   Hector Tobar, "The Politics of Anger" *The Los Angeles Times Magazine* 3 Jan. 1993.

42   Interview with Katie Couric, NBC. The transcript of this interview can be found on the MSNBC website at, http://www.msnbc.com/news/820146.asp. This website was reviewed on 9 Feb. 2003.

43   Peggy Noonan, *What I Saw at the Revolution: A Political Life in the Reagan Era* (New York: Ballantine Books, 1990).

44   Charles Earle Funk, *Heavens to Betsy! and Other Curious Sayings* (New York: HarperCollins Publishers, 2002).

Chapter 6

45   Janice Weinman, Speech at AAUW Convention, June 1997.

46   Interview with Ida Castro, former Exec Director EEOC, National Women's Political Caucus Convention, Houston, Texas, August 1997.

Chapter 7

47   Interview with Marie Wilson, Executive Director, Ms. Foundation at the National Women's Political Caucus Convention, Houston, Texas, August 1997.

48   Charlotte Beers, CEO and Chair of the Board, Ogilvy and Mather, "A New Agenda" *Working Woman*, Nov 1992: 59.

49   J.D. Zahniser, *And Then She Said . . . : Quotations by Women for Every Occasion*, 2nd Ed. (St. Paul: Caillech Press, 1990) 63.

Chapter 8

50   http://www.rice.edu/armadillo/Texas/Jordan/quotes.html. Harvard University Commencement Address, 16 June 1977. The website was reviewed on 20 Jan. 2003.

Chapter 9

51   Lorraine Davis, "Between us: When to speak out!" *VOGUE*, June 1987.

52   Hillary Clinton, remarks at the Democratic National Convention, August 14, 2000. Originally viewed at http://www.abc.com.

53   Gloria Steinem, Smith College Commencement speech, 21 May 1995.

54   Laura Groppe, speech at the National Women's Political Caucus Convention, Houston, Texas, August 1997.

55   Sandie Barnard, *Rise Up: A New guide to Public Speaking* (Ontario: Prentice Hall, 1993): 77. This passage is excerpted from an interview with Gloria Steinem as it is recounted in this book.

Chapter 10

56   Zahniser, *And then she said . . .* , 18.

57   Janey Rifkin, "Women in the Workplace: Bringing Vision, Passion, and Her Inspiration to Hispanic Marketing," *HispanicTimes*, 21.1 (31 Jan. 2000): 26.

58   http://secretary.state.gov/www/picw/index.html. This website is sponsored by The President's Interagency Council on Women, White House Website, reviewed in March 2000.

59   http://secretary.state.gov/www/picw/index.html.

60   Lynette Clemetson and Allison Samuels, "We Have the Power," *Newsweek*, 18 Sept. 2000: 60.

61   Dorothy S. Boulware, "Local UAW Elects First Black, Female VP", *Baltimore Afro-American*, 109.14 (17 Nov. 2000): B9.

62   Patrisia Macias Rojas, "Storming Denver: Padres Unidos Battles for Better Education", *Color Lines*, 3.2 (Summer 2000): 28+.

63   Pamela Newkirk, "Black Journalists," *The Washington Post* 24 Sept. 2000: B03.

64   Margie K. Kitano, "Lessons from Gifted Women of Color," *The Journal of Secondary Gifted Education* 6.2 (Winter 1994–1995): 176–187.

65   Alan Bernstein, "Ethical Ideals of Jordan Won Respect," *Houston Chronicle* 18 Jan. 1996: 1. This passage quotes Stephen Klineberg, a Rice University sociologist.

66   Yong Sheng Xuan, *The Dragon Lover and Other Chinese Proverbs* (California: Shen's Books, 1999).

67   Ela Dutt, "On the Hill: Priya Dayananda: Aide who nurses ambitions of running for Congress", *India Abroad*, XXX.34 (19 May 2000): 14.

68   Spender; *Women of Ideas*; Karlyn Kohrs Campbell, *Man Cannot Speak For Her*, Volumes I and II, (New York: Praeger Publishers, 1988); Scileppi Kennedy and Hartmann O'Shields, *We Shall Be Heard*.

69   Oprah Winfrey, "Commencement Address", Wellesley College, May 30, 1997. Wellesley.edu/public affairs/Winfrey.

70   Wilma Mankiller, Former Chief of the Cherokee Nation, "Rebuilding the Cherokee Nation," speaking at Sweet Briar College, April 2, 1993.

71   Hon. Alexis Herman, "Statement at Swearing in Ceremony," Vital Issues, *The Journal of African American Speeches*, U.S. Department of Labor, Vol. 22, 9 May 1997.

72   Gregory Von Dare, "A Woman Involved: CRISTINA SARALEGUI", *American Woman Road & Travel*, 2000, Caldwell Communications Inc.

73   This quote was found at the following website, http://womens history.about.com/library/qu/blquange.htm. This website was reviewed on 9 Feb. 2003.

Section Four
Chapter 11

74   The History Channel, Anita Hill Speech to Senate Judiciary Committee, The History Channel. 18 Jan 03 http://www. historychannel.com.

75   Cheris Kramerae, Women and Men Speaking (Massachusetts: Newbury House, 1981): xiii.

76   Senator Barbara Boxer, "A New Agenda," *Working Woman* Nov 1992: 61.

77   Elizabeth Kaye, "The Face of Power," *Working Woman* Oct. 1993: 50.

78   Mary Field Belenky, Blythe McVicker Clinchy, Nancy Rule Goldberger, and Jill Mattuck Tarule, *Women's Ways of Knowing: The Development of Self, Voice, and Mind* (New York: Basic Books, Inc, 1986).

79   *NWPC Newsletter*, December 2002.

80   Malcolm Gladwell, *The Tipping Point*, (New York: Little Brown & Co., 2000): 38.

81   Betty Friedan, *The Feminine Mystique* (New York: W.W. Norton & Company, Reprint edition, 1997).

82   Published in *Women in Education*, (—: Bortolussi Publications, 1980).

83   OD Network of *Los Angeles Newsletter*, 1990.

84   Dan Poynter, *Is there a book inside you?* (Santa Barbara, CA: Para Publishing, 1985).

Chapter 12

85   Advokaadiburoo Tak & Co Law Offices, Legal History in Estonia, www.tarkco.com/history.html, 1.

86   Peter Senge, *The Fifth Discipline: The Art and Practice of The Learning Organization* (New York: Doubleday, 1994).

87   Jeannine Stein, "Going to Xtremes (sic): XS and XL," *Los Angeles Times* 2 June 2000: E1-E3.

88   Barbara Mintzer, *Thriving in the Midst of Change* (Georgia: James and Brookfield Publishers, 2002).

Section Five
Appendix

89   Senate OKs 'Partial-Birth' Abortion Ban, *WASHINGTON*, March 13, 2003. This article appeared on the following CBS News website: http://www.cbsnews.com/stories/2003/01/21/politics/printable537275.shtml.

90   Grant McCool, "Teens Edge Away From Traditional Gender Roles" 10 Nov 1999. This information was found on the following website: http://dailynews.yahoo.com/h/nm/19991110/od/life_youth_1.html.

91   Http://secretary.state.gov/www/picw/index.html. The President's Interagency Council on Women website, White House. This website was viewed in March, 2000.

92   The Directory of National Trade and Professional Associations of the *U.S,*(—: Columbia Books, 2002).

93   D.E.Friedman, 'Why the Glass Ceiling?" *Across the Board*, 7 (1988): 33–37.

94   S.G. Haynes & M. Feinleib, "Women, Work and Coronary Heart Disease: Prospective Findings from the Framingham Heart Study," *American Journal of Public Health*, 70 (1980): 133–141.

95   *Women in Higher Education* (July 1997):5. This is referencing an article in the Boston Globe on 27 May 1997.

96   This information was found on the following website: http://www.cimt.luc.edu/womenandtechnology/docs/trends.pdf. It was reviewed on 18 Feb. 2003.

97   Kedric Francis, "Women CEO's: Leading business to the future." *OC Metro* 15 July 1999: 34–42. This is referencing a UCLA dissertation by Suzanne Marshall on women-run businesses.

98   Wiley Hall III, "Tolerance of Bigotry Has Run Out" *LA Times* 11 May 1990.

99   Patrick M. Reilly, "Watchword of Newspaper Publishers At Conference Is Audience Diversity," *Wall Street Journal* 10 May 1991.

100 Jenny Johnson, National Women's Political Caucus, personal email to Anita Perez Ferguson, 11 Dec. 2002.

101 Anna Greenberg, "A Gender Divided: Women as Voters in the 2000 Presidential Election", *Women's Policy Journal of Harvard,* Summer 2001 / Vol. I.

102 http://www.Women.com, This website was reviewed in April 2000. Link to the survey results.

103 Grant McCool, "Teens Edge Away From Traditional Gender Roles" 10 Nov 1999. This information was found on the following website: http://dailynews.yahoo.com/h/nm/19991110/od/life_youth_1.html.

104 e-mail wire service from *jmad@clipper.net;* Progress?. . .a threat to endanger gender equity provisions".

105 "Elite Universities Deny Tenure: Is This a Pattern of Bias or What?" *Women in Higher Education* 5.7 July 1997: 5.

106 Allan Fisher and Jane Margolis, School of Computer Science at Carnegie Mellon University, Women in Computer Sciences: Closing the Gender Gap in Higher Education from Unlocking the Clubhouse: Women in Computing , MIT Press, 2002 found at http://www-2.cs.cmu.edu/~gendergap.

107 "Title IX Hearings Not Encouraging," Michael Dobie, Newsday, February 4, 2003:A24.

108 This information can be found at the website for The President's Interagency Council on Women located at http://secretary.state.gov/www/picw/index.html. This site was reviewed on 9 Feb. 2003.

109 Steven A. Holmes, "Survey Finds Race-Relations Gap In Armed Services, Despite Gains." *The New York Times* 23 Nov. 1999.

110 Refer to the website of Computer Professionals for Social Responsibility at: http://www.cpsr.org/program/gender/index.html.

111 These statistics can be found at http://www.catalystwomen.org/press_room/factsheets/factswbd99.htm. This website was reviewed on 18 Feb. 2003.

112   Ida Castro, "Q: Should women be worried about the glass ceiling in the workplace? Yes: In the corporate world women are scarce at the top and battle a stubborn wage gap" *Insight* 10 Feb. 1997: 24.

113   Elizabeth Becker, "Motherhood Deters Women From Army's Highest Ranks," *The New York Times* 29 Nov. 1999.

114   Michelle Meadows, "Measuring the Distance," AAUW *Outlook*, 92.2 (1998): 6.

115   *SEXUAL HARASSMENT CLAIMS STEP-BY-STEP* by Dale Callender. Copyright) 1998 by Barron's Educational Series, Inc. Published by arrangement with Barron's Educational Series, Inc.

116   *National Policy and Resource Center on Women and Aging*, Volume 1: Number 6, November 1996.

117   *Nursing Homes and Home Care*,by Henry M. Wieman M.D. 11/18/98. These lecture notes were found on the following website: http://family.georgetown.edu/geriatrics/syllabus/index.html.

Index

Authors

Lois Phillips, Ph.D., was the founding executive director of Antioch University Santa Barbara. Her doctoral degree from UCSB focused on gender differences in public speaking. She has also produced and hosted two television shows about women's issues, co-hosted a public radio talk show about current events in Southern California. Her consulting practice focuses on Facilitation of Public Meetings, Board Retreats and Strategic Planning Processes. She also trains and coaches executives, managers, and politicians in organizational communication and presentation skills.

Dr. Phillips has participated in Betty Friedan's Think Tank regarding Women and Public Policy, sponsored by USC's School of Management. She was an "American Feminist in Residence" at Loyola of Concordia University Montreal for a program about the changing roles of women and men. She has appeared with and interviewed Betty Friedan, Germaine Greer, Jane Fonda in public lectures and on television. Producer of "Mother, Daughter, Choices," a documentary for The Girls Club, she has won awards for her work in affirmative action, community leadership, and commitment to education. She has been described as a dynamic speaker who practices what she teaches.

Anita Perez Ferguson, M.A. Management and M.A. Counseling Psychology, is currently a Visiting Lecturer for the Woodrow Wilson Foundation in Princeton, N.J. and the Latin America Trainer/Consultant for Vital Voices Global Partnership in Washington, DC. She also serves on the national board of directors for the Planned Parenthood Federation of America. Her first book entitled *A Passion for Politics* is available on Amazon.com.

Perez Ferguson is past president of the National Women's Political Caucus in Washington, DC. She twice received the Democratic nomination for the US House of Representatives, and made history as the first Hispanic woman in California to run for the US Congress. She served as National Director of Training at the Democratic National Committee and the White House Liaison to the US Department of Transportation. She has presented at Harvard University's JFK School of Government, the American Political Science Association, the League of Women Voters, and the International Platform Association.

Her current focus as a professional speaker and doctoral student at Fielding Graduate Institute includes diversity and governance issues. More information can be found through the American Program Bureau.